JAMES RAWLINGS SYDNOR

THE TRAINING OF CHURCH CHOIRS

ABINGDON (A) PRESS

NEW YORK — NASHVILLE

MT88
.S98

CONTENTS

CONTENTS

INTRODUCTION

After a long career of visiting and helping choirs across England, Sir Walford Davies, Master of the King's Musick, wrote these words: ". . . one thing is significantly certain: whatever the vocal resources may be, you will never find a bad choir where there is a good choirmaster. . . ." [1] Since I also believe this to be true, I have written this little book to help make "good choirmasters."

Enormous satisfaction can be had by choir directors as they work week by week with their choristers *if* they possess technical knowledge and skill. These directors of amateur adult church choirs have the most varied of backgrounds. Most of them play some kind of musical instrument. A number have sung in high-school and college choral groups. Some have had adequate private voice instruction. A few could be called professional soloists. An overwhelming majority of them bring enthusiasm and eagerness to their task of choir management. They know that as the choral work is improved, to that extent their church is better able to serve the congregation.

Yet these amateur choirmasters have not been through the well-rounded curriculum of a choir college. They may never have had even a week's course in choral methods in a summer conference. With this limited technical facility, they manage the one group of the church which must report each week to the entire congregation on the

[1] *Music and Worship*, p. 241.

thoroughness of its preparation and on its general competence. This pressure can either produce continued embarrassment or can prove to be a challenge to provide the finest kind of leadership in worship.

Three considerations have guided the author in preparing this manual. First, the material on these pages is designed to help train adult amateur church choirs. Since much of the information deals with basic choral technique, it can be adapted for youth and children.

Second, I have assumed no previous specific instruction in choir technique. Obviously, any past music experience —passive or active—will feed into one's present choral endeavors. Indeed, any ability at organizing group experience will assist.

Third, I will try to introduce the reader to the essential facts regarding choir training. I hope to acquaint him with the means for giving deep-seated joy to his choristers, the congregation, and himself as they make music in the house of God. This book is small in compass, however. On my study shelves there are books of several hundred pages devoted to just one of the dozens of topics covered in this introductory manual. Since the subject obviously cannot be exhausted in the scope of this volume, I trust that the list of books at the end will furnish a guide to further exploration.

In the final analysis, experience in the choir room must supplement and confirm instruction. Experienced golfers know the value of a well-organized book about golf and of the help of the golf pro, but they also have discovered that the game is really learned on the tee, the fairway, and the green—with abundant trips into the rough! So it is with choir work. As Dr. Ralph Vaughan Williams wrote, "Conducting can, however, only be learnt at the conductor's desk."

CHAPTER I

About Church Choirs--
Their Background and Purpose

In the divine economy God has given special gifts to his children. The apostle Paul in I Cor. 12:27-31 wrote that God appointed apostles, prophets, teachers, healers. The recipients of these spiritual gifts enabled the newly founded church to flourish. To many Christians through the ages he has given musical talent which by training and practice can be used in his worship.

This singling out of experienced singers and using them in divine praise even antecedes the Christian Era. In II Chr. 5:13 we read of an early Hebrew use wherein "the trumpeters and singers were as one, to make one sound to be heard in praising and thanking the Lord."

Beginning in the fourth century we can trace the story of the church's music as sung by its choirs. At the time of Pope Sylvester I in the early fourth century, a group of singers called *schola cantorum* is presumed to have existed. This early record could be considered the beginning of the pontifical singers who later became the famed Sistine Choir of the Roman Church, served by such musicians as Palestrina, Nanini, and Allegri.

Another choir of ancient rootage is the Chapel Royal of the British Crown whose records go back to 1135. Modern choir directors might envy a prerogative of this famous royal choir. Under Richard III (1483-85) representatives of the Chapel could travel about the country, listening to the cathedral choirs and robbing them of any boys whose voices were fit to sing before the King! The roster of its musicians includes many of the famous names of British musical history such as Tallis, Byrd, Gibbons, and Purcell.

We will take space just to mention examples of the variety and richness of the Church's choral tradition[1]—the inspired tuition of the choristers in Saint Thomas Church in Leipzig by the great cantor Johann Sebastian Bach, the cathedral choirs of Britain with their magnificent choral literature, the children's choir movement which is spreading throughout the world, the enormous increase of volunteer youth and adult choirs in our land. From the lips of these unnumbered choristers praises with understanding have arisen to Almighty God.

The Purpose of Choirs in Church

The primary function of the choir is to join with all other members of the congregation in offering worship to Almighty God and, in so doing, to lead the congregation in worship through hymns, anthems, and in the sung portions of the liturgy.

As leaders in worship, the choir exercises two functions which need to be kept in proper balance—the priestly and the prophetic. The first is emphasized in some denominations; in others the prophetic role is kept to the fore.[2]

Just as the minister in his public prayers leads the congregation through the experiences of praise, confession,

[1] The details of choir history are scattered through general histories of music. Sir Sydney Nicholson in *Quires and Places Where They Sing* has a chapter on "Choirs of Olden Times." A good recent history of choral music of the past five centuries is Dr. Percy M. Young's *The Choral Tradition* which is a historical and analytical survey.

[2] Charles Cleall in his book *The Selection and Training of Mixed Choirs in Churches* discusses these two functions at some length.

8

gratitude, petition, and dedication, so the choir through the sung prayers does the same. As John Calvin wrote, "As to the public prayers, these are of two kinds: some are offered by means of words alone, the others with song." [3] When a choir sings Samuel Sebastian Wesley's wonderful, simple setting of Ps. 5:8; 4:8, "Lead me, Lord," not only do the choristers offer for themselves this prayer for guidance, but the congregation also lifts its heart as this sung prayer is heard. As the choir sings its praise in Brahms's "How lovely is Thy dwellingplace, O Lord of Hosts" the congregation, paying reverent attention, receives a new vision of the blessedness of the Courts of the Lord.

A notable illustration of this priestly choral activity was the singing of the choir of Saint Paul's Cathedral on May 24, 1738. This was the day when John Wesley was so moved by the singing that at the end of the day he recorded the entire text of the anthem in his *Journal*. The words were as follows:

Out of the deep have I called unto thee, O Lord. O let thine ears consider well the voice of my complaint. If thou, Lord, wilt be extreme to mark what is done amiss, O Lord, who may abide it? For there is mercy with thee; therefore shalt thou be feared. O Israel, trust in the Lord: for with the Lord there is mercy, and with him is plenteous redemption. And he shall redeem Israel from all his sins.

If we know that this was the memorable day when his heart was "strangely warmed" we realize that this singing of Ps. 130 had been his own prayer. From the experiences

[3] Foreword to Geneva Psalter, 1543. Translation from Strunk, *Source Readings in Music History* (New York: W. W. Norton & Company, 1950), p. 346.

9

of these late May days in 1738, John and Charles Wesley went out to evangelize Britain.

In addition to this priestly role, a choir fulfils a prophetic ministry. A scriptural basis for this may be read in I Cor. 14. It could be summed up in the vs. 19: "Nevertheless, in church I would rather speak five words with my mind, in order to instruct others, than ten thousand words in a tongue." Through the truths of the anthem texts a choir can interpret the Christian gospel. A glance at a list of choir music may reveal titles like Holst's "Turn back, O man, forswear thy foolish ways," and Thatcher's "Come, ye faithful, raise the strain," both of which are addressed to the worshipers. In Paul's words, the choir teaches and admonishes with psalms, hymns, and spiritual songs (Col. 3:16).

An additional reason for the choir's existence in many churches is its encouragement and guidance given to congregational singing. Choir members presumably have more native musical talent. They certainly have opportunity for rehearsal. They know more about reading music notation. Therefore, their confidence and freedom of expression will be a positive example during hymn singing and other acts of corporate musical worship. This is why John Wesley advised the congregation to "attend close to the leading voices, and move therewith as exactly as you can." Not only can the choristers add spirit to the singing of familiar hymns but they also can demonstrate the melodies of unfamiliar hymns through outlining the melody in unison or by singing hymn anthems. John Calvin introduced the new psalter tunes in Geneva by having his musician Louis Bourgeois teach the melodies to the children of the congregation—at one hour's rehearsal a day—who in turn instructed the congregation.

Another genuine value of church choirs is the educational and recreational opportunities offered the singers. The development of skill in the use of the singing voice, the re-creation of some of the world's most exalted music, the formation of close friendships in artistic endeavor, the opportunity to serve in the church's worship and work —these and many other benefits acrue to choristers who are members of an enterprising choir. And permeating all should be the pure pleasure of making music. Calvin expressed it this way, "Now among the other things proper to recreate man and give him pleasure, music is either the first or one of the principal, and we must think that it is a gift of God deputed to that purpose." [4]

Choristers and their directors are called to serve in the most crucial institution in the world today. They should realize and be committed to the truth expressed in the words of the Reverend A. C. Craig of Scotland: ". . . the ultimate realism is not the realism of power-politics, nor the realism of nationalistic self-interest, but discernment of, and obedience to, the Will of God revealed in the Event of Jesus Christ—His life and teaching, His dying and rising from the dead, His reigning in heaven and His presence on earth by His Holy Spirit." [5]

Church musicians are called to be Christ's musicians.

[4] Geneva Psalter, *op. cit.*, p. 347.
[5] *The British Weekly* (June 1, 1961), p. 1.

11

CHAPTER **II**

Three Characteristics
of the Church Choir Director

The crux of the problem of developing fine choirs for our churches is the training of highly skilled choral directors. Because this is the most important fact in choir training, we are going to set forth three basic qualifications (there are others) for success in this enterprise, before we move into the following chapters on practical techniques.

1. *The choir director in a local congregation should understand and be deeply committed to the faith of his church.*

Truly artistic endeavor springs from a spirit which has integrity. Its basic desire is to communicate the insights of beauty and meaning which were bestowed by inspiration and hard work. In a real sense, then, all pursuit of beauty and order is religious in nature.

Most readers of these pages serve as musicians in congregations whose creeds are in the Protestant tradition. To interpret the realities of the Christian faith to the choirs and through them to the congregation means not only knowledge of the fundamentals of doctrine but also devotion to the Author and Finisher of the faith, Jesus Christ.

The major reason Johann Sebastian Bach was the inspired giant of Protestant music was the fact that he was a diligent lifelong student of Christian doctrine. In the *Specification of the Estate Left by the Late Mr. Johann*

Sebastian Bach, Chapter XII, under the heading "Sacred Books," there were fifty-two separate items listed including such books as fifteen volumes of Luther's works, Stenger's *Foundations of the Augsburg Confession,* Bible commentaries, and sermon collections.[1] He knew the foundations of his faith.

His devotion to his personal Lord is apparent to anyone who studies and loves his musical commentaries on the Christian faith shown in his numerous cantatas, passions, and especially in the monumental Mass in B Minor. His underlying religious motive is shown by the Latin phrase appended to his manuscripts—*Soli Deo Gloria,* "To God alone be the glory."

A wholesome sign on the church-music horizon is the increasing number of articles in professional journals on the relationship of theology and music, written not just by theologians but by practicing competent musicians. Church musicians of today should devote a shelf of their libraries to works of theological exposition. Among their professional mentors should be men like Paul Tillich, John and Donald Baillie, and Reinhold Niebuhr.

Ages ago a sage said that everyone can be eloquent on a subject he understands. The church musician can speak eloquently about the gospel through his music and his life to the extent to which he understands and experiences the newness and amplitude of life in Christ.

2. *A choir director should assess and accept his unique abilities and situation.*

The profession of church choir directing is filled with a most varied group of people. Unlike the medical or legal profession, there are, as a rule, no prerequisites

[1] For complete list, see Hans David and Arthur Mendel, *The Bach Reader* (New York: W. W. Norton & Company, 1945), pp. 195-96.

of collegiate and graduate professional study. With few exceptions there are no licensing examinations such as exist in the state bar and medical associations. A choir director may be the mother of four youngsters—subject to the usual measles and chickenpox—who may have sung in the college choir for two years and who directs the choir because "there simply wasn't anyone else to do it!" Another choirmaster may have his doctorate in sacred music and may have spent several years studying abroad. He may have the finest in rehearsal and instrumental facilities and may be able to devote undivided time and attention to his music making. We could go on to sketch a large variety of persons and situations in this field, but the fact is apparent that a large diversity is present in the profession of choir trainers.

Since this is so, it is of paramount importance to recall that growth in professional competence begins with a realistic appraisal of one's unique abilities and working situation. The director may recall with nostalgia the magnificent unaccompanied motets he sang in the university glee club and may yearn to use them in the Sunnyside Church in Mechanicsville. But there is a vast difference between a choir handpicked from a student body of four thousand collegians, with the lure of a long spring tour down East, and with rehearsals three times weekly, and the choir at Sunnyside, where there are fourteen singers, mostly nonreaders. There the singers are parents with children who get sick; they are rehearsed one or two hours at the fag end of the day. Common sense tells one that the grade—but not the quality!—of music sung and the methods used must be adapted to the particular situation. A prayer phrased by Reinhold Niebuhr is appropriate for all choir directors, "God, grant me the serenity to accept things I cannot change, courage to change things I can, and wisdom to know the difference."

The director of the college choir is somewhat like a scientist giving a seminar in nuclear physics. The director of Sunnyside Church choir is like the teacher of a one-room school teaching grades one through six. The village director may have two excellent music readers, several music illiterates, and "Miss Whooper, Mrs. Slightly-Sharp, Mr. Shaker Flop, and Dr. Rasper." [2]

Here lies the excitement, the newness of the task. You bring ingenuity and imagination to problems unlike any other in the wide world. Every choir can be a good choir within its unique limitations. There are beautiful, expressive, simple anthems which can be well sung by any hard-working, competently directed choir.

The choir director can and should be himself. Indeed, if he tries unduly to imitate others or if he wastes time envying another situation, he will only create inner tensions. Christian realism begins with accepting the fact that we are fallible human beings but that, in the service of Christ, we can confidently expect the guidance of the Holy Spirit in all decisions and actions.

3. *The choir director should expect continued professional growth and should plan for it.*

Choir directors can learn from the example of the greatest Protestant church musician, Johann Sebastian Bach. Speaking of Bach's influence on his students, Spitta wrote: "He set the highest value on industry, and set himself up as an example to them in this alone. 'I have to be diligent,' he would say, 'and anyone who is equally

[2] Charles Cleall's picturesque terms in *The Selection and Training of Mixed Choirs in Churches* (London: The Independent Press, Ltd., 1960), p. 94.

so will get on equally well.' He never seemed to be aware of his wonderful gifts." [3]

In long-range planning for personal growth it is wise to discover one's strong points, and also the greatest gaps in one's professional equipment. Do you have special trouble in working with groups? There is a good deal of literature and instruction available on group psychology and interpersonal relationships. Do you know much about the human voice, its training and use? Have you made special study of musical interpretation and styles? How about techniques for developing music reading facility in your choir? Think of the hours it would save over teaching by rote. Do you know the history and principles of Christian worship as channeled through your denomination? Are children's choirs your weakest spot?

You cannot learn all these things at once, but you can begin, and the pilgrimage of learning will be rewarding. Scores of church-music workshops are held across the country. Summer conferences are listed in professional journals each spring. The number of good books on the subject of choir directing is increasing. The bibliography at the end of this book could be a guide to developing a personal working professional library.

I have written at some length on the subject of in-service training for church musicians in *Planning for Church Music*.[4]

[3] Philipp Spitta, *Johann Sebastian Bach* (New York: Dover Publication, 1951), II, 50.

[4] Nashville: Abingdon Press, 1961, pp. 21-29.

CHAPTER III

The Director and His Choristers

The caliber of the individual choristers will largely determine the quality of the choral endeavor in a specific church, just as the pipework of the organ—its voicing and placement—is determinative in the king of instruments. The challenging distinction is obvious. The choral instrument is living, susceptible of amazing growth or deadening stagnation.

The principal attraction to a choir will be excellent, varied music well sung. Word gets around that an expenditure of time and effort in a particular choir will yield the satisfaction of an artistic enterprise well done. The fellowship, the opportunity of service to the church, the personality of the director, the technical growth—these also attract people to the choir.

Many means are used to secure singers. Personal contacts between director and prospects are best. However, potential singers can be discovered by periodic notices, varied in text, in the church bulletins which ask interested individuals to speak to the director after the service or to call him by phone. Choir members, music-committee members, the minister, and other staff personnel can be on the lookout for choir potential. Many directors attend the orientation meetings for new church members and explain available choral activities in the congregation. Booklets are sometimes provided describing the choral groups, their programs, rehearsal times, ages, and similar information. The conductor of the local choral society sometimes can provide names of new singers who have not yet affiliated with any congregation. Voice teachers are willing sometimes to suggest names of their pupils.[1]

Auditions

I firmly believe in auditions for membership in church choirs. It is as reasonable to screen applicants for choirs as to check on the mathematical potential and competence of applicants for a team of auditors. The director can evaluate the vocal and musical abilities. Also this conference between director and applicant gives opportunity to assess the character and personality traits of the would-be chorister. The esprit de corps of a choir can be strengthened by a vital, bouyant, new singer or can be seriously troubled by a crackpot.

The church authorities must realize that the historic church has generally provided two basic levels of music endeavor—amateur and expert. The first is represented by the hymnal and by congregational singing. This requires no special musical skill or rehearsal. Plenty of Christians who cannot even carry a tune praise God in hymn singing, and their praise is acceptable to him. The second kind of music making is done by vocalists and instrumentalists who have some native talent and who are willing to devote time and effort to music practice. Some church members have neither qualification; they should not be in the choir.

If a dubious or timid choir director wishes to struggle with this problem further there are a number of excellent extensive debates available. Donald Kettring has devoted

[1] Charles Heaton in *How to Build a Church Choir* (St. Louis: Bethany Press, 1958) discusses further methods of procuring new members.

twelve pages to this subject in his *Steps Toward a Singing Church*. Charles Cleall has a stimulating book with forthright positions regarding auditions.[2]

This does not mean that the applicant must have superb tone and be able to read a motet part unaccompanied at sight. But it does mean that the applicant is willing to attend rehearsals and services regularly and to work hard at the task of becoming a chorister "who needeth not to be ashamed." I have had eager singers with normal vocal ability but with no music reading ability to speak of who developed into valuable singers.

During the audition the director will attempt to put the applicant at ease. After some preliminary conversation, the director might suggest that the person sing a simple hymn tune with a moderate range. Next, if the person has sung parts before, he or she could be asked to sing, say, the alto or bass part of this hymn. If he is extremely timid or uncertain the director could sing along on the part, gradually lightening the volume in order to hear the singer. It is wise, too, to test the ability of this person to sing a melody while the director sings another part against it to see whether an independent part can be maintained. Some ear testing can be done such as sounding two different pitches in succession at the piano or voice and asking the applicant which is higher. A simple three part chord can be sounded and the person asked to sing each of the three tones. The range can be discovered by vocalizing scales on a vowel. Various volume levels should be tried to ascertain quality at these levels. A written record of the findings should be made at this time or immediately after the audition.

[2] *The Selection and Training of Mixed Choirs in Churches*, pp. 88-89, 103.

The director may decide on the basis of this conference whether it is wise to admit this person to full membership in the choir. If so, the individual is told then and there. Sometimes the suggestion is made that the person try choir attendance for a month, during which time the director and the singer can see what progress has been made. After this probation period a final decision can be rendered. There are some choirs which require each singer to audition every several years.

In auditions, one must balance a concern for the individual, the choir, and the congregation.

The new chorister could be given a copy of Carl Halter's helpful little booklet *The Christian Choir Member*.[3]

Classification of Voices

Although we shall discuss the singing voice in a later chapter, we should describe at this point certain aspects of the classification procedure. One of the soundest statements on this problem which has come to the writer's attention was developed by the American Academy of Teachers of Singing. Founded in 1922, this is a small group of representative and nationally known teachers of singing. The Academy's publications are the result of intensive and extensive study by committees whose reports are given critical consideration by the entire membership. On approval by a majority, these reports, in the form of pronouncements and song lists, are published.[4]

Its pronouncement on the *Classification of the Singing*

[3] St. Louis: Concordia Publishing House, 1959.

[4] Academy publications may be secured from Harold C. Luckstone, Secretary, 57 Winter Street, Forest Hills 75, New York. A list is available.

Voice, issued in 1956, is a four-page leaflet giving nine propositions which are succinctly discussed. In the interest of brevity, only the headings—with a few exceptions—are here given. Readers are urged to secure and study the entire statement. Here are the excerpts:

1. The kind of voice possessed by any individual is a gift of nature and its basic potential cannot be altered. . . .

2. The kind of voice possessed by any individual is determined by the size and proportions of the vocal mechanism. . . .

3. It is not essential that the teacher make a classification of a voice at a first hearing.

In some voices, especially those of young beginners, the type of voice is not indicated at the start of study. In such cases it is wiser not to make a final classification of the voice until sufficient training has unmistakably revealed it. A temporary classification may be made and future probabilities noted in such cases, but it is advisable to avoid fixing in the mind of the student any particular voice type because the emergence of the true potential may be retarded thereby.

The first decision of the teacher should be whether the voice is properly used and whether the trend is high or low. . . .

4. Vocal range alone is a most unreliable and deceiving factor in determining voice type. . . .

5. The tessitura that the developed, trained voice is capable of maintaining successfully is an excellent, final test of proper voice classification. . . .

6. Virtuoso voices can perform extreme feats. . . .

7. Correct voice classification is particularly important when assigning young singers to the voice parts in a chorus. When the class of a singer's voice is not clearly defined, or where there is a question as to which of two sections of a chorus should be chosen, it is generally better to put the singer in the lower rather than the higher of two possible parts in order to avoid voice strain, always with the under-

standing that such assignment is tentative and subject to change as the voice develops and its true potential emerges. . . .

8. Voice classifications. There are six major voice classifications generally recognized. These are soprano, mezzo-soprano, contralto, tenor, baritone and bass. . . .

9. Aural tests. Various aural tests are used by teachers and schools of singing to determine the type of voice. . . . Such practices or tests, however successful they may be in the hands of the experienced teacher cannot be presented in a formula to be employed by any reader successfully. The American Academy of Teachers of Singing believes that the decision as to the type of voice must depend, primarily, on the judgment of the experienced, skillful teacher.[5]

In an earlier pronouncement (1944) the Academy discussed the *Problems of Tessitura in Relation to Choral Music.* As indicated in item 5 above, this factor is an excellent test for determining voice classification. The Academy states:

In this connection the designation TESSITURA, or "heart of the range," is used in accordance with the definition given by *Grove's Dictionary* as "the prevailing or AVERAGE position of the notes in relation to the compass of the voice, whether high, low or medium," and is not to be confused with the word RANGE. In the following tabulations the vocal limits allocated to the various voices are those of the AVERAGE AMATEUR SINGER and not the professional artist, and refer *only* to CHORAL MUSIC.

Then the Academy gives the following notations to show "the safest and best RANGE and the safest and best TESSITURA for the various voices:—(The TESSITURA limitations do not prohibit the composer

[5] Used by permission.

22

and arranger from writing for the full RANGE of the voice.)"

VOICE		RANGE	TESSITURA
First Soprano	(D) E to G (A flat)		A - D
Second Soprano (Mezzo)	C to F		G - C
Alto	(G) A flat to C (D)		(2 Tessiture) Upper - F - B♭ / Lower A - D
First Tenor	(D) E to F sharp (G)		A - D
Second Tenor	(C) D to E (F)		F♯ - C
Baritone	A to D		D - A
Bass	(E) F to B (C)		(2 Tessiture) Upper E♭ - A♭ / Lower F - B♭

NOTE: If composers and arrangers would keep within the suggested RANGE and favor the recommended TESSITURA, voices will be protected and the choral music will be more effective when performed.[6]

---

[6] Used by permission.

CHAPTER IV

The Director's Understanding
of Choral Music Notation

We will repeatedly say that the ease and rapidity with which a choir can be taught music is in direct proportion to the clarity with which the director perceives the composer's intent. Although the notational system which has been developed through the centuries is a marvelous instrument for portraying tonal images, it is, nevertheless, imperfect. Liszt said in the directions attached to the score of his "Symphonic Poems," "Although I have tried through exact markings of the dynamics, the accelerations and slowing up of the tempo, to clearly indicate my wishes, I must confess that much, even that which is of the greatest importance cannot be expressed on paper." [1] For this reason it should be helpful to discuss how to understand choral music notation.

First, what is music? Its various language has been described in many glowing passages of literature. For our immediate purpose let us explain it this way. In its simplest form music is *a stream of tone* which flows in time, just as a line of color in a painting exists in space. All musical meaning derives ultimately from the behavior of each contributing stream of tone. The music which exists in a composer's spirit as he attempts to transmit it

[1] Quoted in Albert Stoessel, *The Technic of the Baton* (New York: Carl Fischer, Inc., 1928), p. 5.

in manuscript is composed of these plastic, moving, free streams of living tone.

Some writers, in attempting to express this phenomenon of connected tones, use the analogy of a *line*. For example, Ernest Newman, British music critic, writes of the violin playing of Kreisler or Ysaye: "By his phrasing he makes the melody a series of lines, perfect first of all in their own drawing and then in their relation to each other; by his shading he makes the lines seem to breathe like living things—or, if you prefer to look at it in that way, he adds beauty of colour to their beauty of pure line." [2] The famous interpreter of Scottish folk song, Marjory Kennedy-Fraser, gives this advice, "In studying phrasing, get rid of the picture of the notation as soon as possible, re-creating the melodic line mentally." [3]

Although this conception of musical line is helpful, there is always the implication of something static, fixed. That is why the conception of *stream*, suggesting mobility and freedom, has appealed to other writers. Charles Kennedy Scott, eminent London choral director, says, in writing about style of singing madrigals, "The essence of it is *liquidity* of sound; a supple, continuous flow; the perfection of *legato* though it may take a *staccato* form." [4] Percy Scholes sums it up by saying, ". . . perhaps flow is the greatest foundational quality of good musical performance in any medium." [5]

[2] *Solo Singing*, Festival Booklet #5 (London: Paterson's Publications, Ltd.), p. 3.

[3] *Hebridean Song and the Laws of Interpretation* (London: Paterson's Publications, Ltd.), p. 11. Used by permission of the publisher and Carl Fischer, Inc.

[4] *Madrigal Singing* (London: Oxford University Press), p. 50.

[5] *Oxford Companion to Music*, article on conducting, p. 220. Quotations used by permission.

We gain fresh insight into the real life of music when we learn that the word "rhythm" is derived etymologically from the Greek verb "rhein" meaning "to flow." Musical rhythm, then, has to do with that which flows. Of remarkable significance also is the fact that the word "stream" also has a derivative relation with this same Greek verb. So when we speak of the rhythm of music we should think of *its behavior as a stream of tone*.

Recall some beautiful mountain stream which you have visited. Its forward motion is ever varied, always lovely. After plunging furiously through a narrow gorge, it comes almost to rest in a deep pool under a shading hemlock. Then it flows silently like emerald velvet over a broad carpet of moss. Presently it is dashing over a pebbly bed strewn with random boulders. So its progress to the valley is punctuated by a thousand influences.

Even so, an immortal melody, played or sung for us by an artist, yields a similar sense of beautiful vitality. Its interest and consequent fascination is a result of its intrinsic rhythm. Willan Swainson of Aberdeen describes rhythm in this broad sense: "Musical rhythm is a sense of vitality, progression and balance produced by the influence of duration, speed, and accent upon pitch." [6] In other words, the stream of tone is affected by a series of influences or stresses, just as a mountain stream is altered in width, depth, and behavior. All musicians should understand the kinds and functions of the basic music accents. They are described in *Grove's Dictionary* (See heading Time: Accent) and in many technical works on music substance. Briefly they are:

[6] *Manual of Church Praise According to the Use of the Church of Scotland* (Edinburgh: The Church of Scotland Committee on Publications, 1932), p. 202.

1. *Pitch accent.* Any change of pitch in a melody, up or down, has significance and could produce an accent or stress.

2. *Tonic accent.* Grove says, "The fact that a note is of higher pitch tends to accentuate it, especially in vocal music."

3. *Harmonic accent.* A harmonic accent is the momentary tendency to emphasis given the music by the presence of an unusually significant chord, usually a dissonant one. As Charles Kennedy Scott says, "It has always been recognized that the expressive power of music resides largely in the use of dissonance. . . ." [7]

4. *Agogic accent.* "The longer of two successive notes is said to bear the agogic (or 'attracting') accent," says Grove.

5. *Metrical accent.* A metric accent is the type of emphasis which the first note of each measure tends to have. This is the one kind of stress associated with *regularity*. We shall have more to say of this kind of accent presently.

6. *Dynamic accent.* A dynamic accent is the emphasis given a tone by a momentary increase of volume. This is probably the most commonly used kind of accent.

7. *Qualitative accent.* A qualitative accent is the emphasis which a tone has when the timbre is suddenly changed.

8. *Cumulative accent.* A cumulative accent falls upon a note when the preceding tones are arranged in such a way as to give it emphasis.

Although the implications of each of these accents are profound with respect to choral vitality, I would like to emphasize one—the metric accent. The forward progress of the music is measured by the recurrence of a predictable regular pulse; by this we do not mean a mechanical clubbing of the first note in each measure. This *beat* in music might well be compared to the powerful forward surge of a racing shell propelled by the regular and

[7] *Op. cit.,* p. 27.

simultaneous strokes of many oars. The craft glides smoothly forward and receives a slight additional thrust with each sweep of the oars. Or we can liken it to the sprint of a hundred-yard dasher. His body hurtles through the air but his dash is punctuated by the beat of his feet on the cinder track.

This rhythmic insistence, found in Bach's music, is explained in this significant passage from Dr. Wilibald Gurlitt's book *Johann Sebastian Bach: The Master and His Work*. Speaking of Veit Bach (d. 1619), the miller who was an early ancestor of the famous Bach musical family, Dr. Gurlitt writes:

In regard to his playing of the lute the family chronicle expressly states that its beat, i.e., its rhythm (not the melody), was learned from the uniform sound of the mill wheels and the deep, peaceful currents of the millstream. In the compulsory uniformity of movement provided by the playing of his water mill, the primal Bach seems to have found the characteristic movement of that instrumental and rhythmically strong performance which, 'so to speak, provided the beginning of music among his descendants.' [8]

One of the most fundamental concepts in choral movement is this periodicity of beat. It is this and this alone which enables a choir to stay together. It is ascertained from the gestures of the conductor, the pulse of the accompaniment, and the unwritten agreement "never to stop the march of the song." Not only does this compact between singers and director give reassurance and mutual trust but it has many beneficial by-products, a principal one being crisp enunciation of consonants. For in-

[8] Translated by Oliver C. Rupprecht (St. Louis: Concordia Publishing House, 1957), p. 13.

stance, how in the world can a choir time the enunciation of explosive consonants to the team if the choristers arrive at the instant of explosion at different moments? Instead of a crisp consonant—"T" for example—we would have a barrage of miniature explosions.

The beat in music is as fundamental to efficient choral singing as the inch is essential to the art of architecture. On what other terms could architect, contractor, and carpenter co-operate to produce a substantial and lovely building? A choral conductor can usually discover the unit of beat intended by the composer by looking at the metronome indication at the beginning of the anthem. There you may see $=82$. The time signature may be 3/4, but because of an intended rapid pace, the quarter note is not the unit of beat. The first note in each measure receives the pulse. Likewise a 4/4 signature does not necessarily indicate the quarter-note beat. Quite likely the unit of beat is the half-note, and the metronomic marking would indicate a speed for the half-note unit.

After we have emphasized the need for steadiness of beat in choral singing we should add that any artistic musical performance will reveal to the analytical listener certain fluctuations of tempo not indicated in the score. This elasticity of movement has been commonly known as *tempo rubato*. Webster's *New International Dictionary* explains this musical phenomenon in the following words: "Psychologically, musical rhythm is based on felt muscular response rather than merely upon timed tone lengths and it is this supremacy of the personal response over the mere exactness and regularity of measured time units that makes possible the various subtleties and fluctuations in rhythm and tempo known collectively as *tempo rubato*." Sir Donald Tovey says, "The genuine

29

tempo rubato is, as its name implies, a rhythmic robbing of Peter to pay Paul." [9]

A word of warning should be given about the careless use of tempo rubato. There is a great deal of "expression" which is ill-proportioned and unrhythmical. All musicians should heed Marjory Kennedy-Fraser's advice concerning its use:

Only those who can sing strictly in time can be trusted with *tempo rubato* deviation and return. We must live under the law before we can live under grace! Never try to *make* rubato effects—a good rubato is never in evidence. It must curve so naturally from slow into faster and *vice versa* that only an expert watching for it is aware that it has been used. [10]

Percy Scholes in his *Oxford Companion to Music* has a two-page article on rubato, and he restricts its meaning to the "give-and-take" within a limited unit of the time scheme. He does not consider mere flexibility of general tempo the definition of our term. He confines its meaning to the deviation of tempo *within a phrase*.

The eight accents, outlined above, are primarily musical in nature. We should mention another type of accent, nonmusical, which vitally affects choral performance—*word accent*. The text of an anthem will have its own movement toward important words of a phrase. For instance, the verse "In the *beginning* was the *Word*" has two points of special significance which would be highlighted in intelligent reading and singing. This is why

[9] From article on rhythm. See his *Musical Articles From the Encyclopaedia Britannica* (London: Oxford University Press, 1944), p. 179.

[10] *Op. cit.*, p. 14. Used by permission of Paterson's Publications, Ltd., and Carl Fischer, Inc.

Charles Kennedy Scott, speaking of madrigal singing, writes: ". . . the cue to right accenting should be always the word and never the bar-line." [11] With this principle in mind, Gustav Holst in "Man born to toil" (G. Schirmer: Choral Church Music, No. 8509) reminds the unwary singer of the location of word and syllable accents by placing stress signs as in the following bars:

Used by permission of G. Schirmer, Inc.

An extension of the principle stated above would lead us to say that not only words and syllables should have intelligent accenting but also word particles, such as consonants, should have occasional stressing. All skillful choral directors know the expressive power of a deftly turned consonant. There is enormous emotional thrust in the choral enunciation of the final *sh* in the word "flash." Directors know the propulsive effect of the initial *B* in a repetitive phrase such as *bonae, bonae voluntatis.*

What Is a Phrase?

The inner meaning of the music is ultimately conveyed by the shape and behavior of the individual phrases. A phrase is a series of related notes. Hans David said:

[11] *Op. cit.*, p. 24.

Each phrase has a certain integrity and unity of line that should be made apparent. Tension may appear in the delivery of an ascending line, and relaxation in the delivery of a descending one, although a definite firmness should be maintained to the very end of the phrase. Each line has a natural center, a turning-point towards which it tends and from which it flows off. This "pivot" is often the highest note of the phrase.[12]

Charles Kennedy Scott qualifies David's last sentence by saying, "As a rule the principal accent of a phrase coincides with both the highest and longest notes."[13] Herman Scherchen gives a significant amplification to David's description of a musical phrase and its execution. In his *Handbook of Conducting* he wrote: "Thus, all singing is concentration and release. Every melody carries its form-giving motion up to a central point, from which point onwards the notes are released. Concentration is tension; tension seems to be *crescendo;* and *crescendo,* conversely, is the music's urge to reach its central point."[14]

From this we see that a phrase is a series of musical tones so arranged in order of importance that a major stress—or concentration of energy—is placed on the climactic note. By extension, any well-constructed piece of music demonstrates in its overall form this same principle of concentration and release. Each phrase occupies its proper place in the construction of minor climaxes, and all together set off the one major event or climax of the whole composition. For example, in Handel's "Hallelujah

[12] *The Art of Polyphonic Song* (New York: G. Schirmer, 1940), p. 12.

[13] *Op. cit.,* p. 55.

[14] London: Oxford University Press, 1933, p. 29.

Chorus" we find a remarkable accumulation of intensity from the phrase:

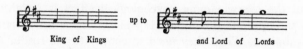

where a tremendous cumulative stress is located. Of the latter phrase, Sir Edward Bairstow says, "This is the main climax, the central tower of this cathedral, as the opening is the western front and the final apotheosis the east end." [15]

Music, simply speaking, is a stream of tone which possesses beauty and interest through the interplay of the elements of pitch, time, volume, and quality. Furthermore, we have found that the significance of this stream of tone lies in its *destination*—where it is going—not only within the phrase but beyond its bounds, within the whole composition.

The Limitations of Music Notation

Yet we must confess that our system of musical notation, excellent as it is, is partly to blame for so much disjunct, unmusical singing. Two aspects of our system of musical notation conspire to confuse the unwary musician: (1) The use of dots instead of lines to represent connected streams of tone, and (2) the presence of bar lines which constitute psychological blocks to forward movement.

Dots. A dot is an isolated phenomenon. Its chief characteristic is its lack of connection with any other like phenomenon. This is the exact opposite of its purpose

[15] *Handel's Oratorio "The Messiah"* (The Musical Pilgrim Series; London: Oxford University Press, 1928), p. 44.

in musical notation. Except for occasional staccato effects, a dot in music should signify that the represented tone is absolutely connected with the succeeding tone. But the overwhelming psychological effect is weighted in the opposite direction. Map makers have used better symbolism. When they need to convey to the reader an idea of a connected phenomenon like a highway or river, they do not use a series of dots; they use lines.

In addition to failing to convey the idea of *connected* tone, dots fail to give anything like an adequate simple idea of the *duration* of the particular tone. A tone twice as long as another is represented by a dot of the same size; e.g., ♩ ♪. Musicians know, of course, that the filled-in note is the shorter, but a reader of music must engage in much more extensive mental process to arrive at this conclusion—memory, association, et cetera—than to observe the obvious proportions of two lines, one twice the length of the other ——— ——————. The line symbols are obviously proportional whereas the dots are not.

This lack of obvious temporal connotation is undoubtedly responsible for the deficiency of "timekeeping" on the part of singers in choruses. As Sir Hugh Roberton wrote, "Remember that for one choir that falls in note mistakes, ten fall in time distortions." [16]

The use of dots fails likewise to give any conception of the volume and quality variation in music. In other words, there is no provision made in the basic symbol of the tone—the dot—for representing these very important factors in the stream of tone. It would be patently impossible to show a phrase crescendo and dimuendo by

[16] *Mixed Voice Choirs* (London: Paterson's Publications, Ltd.), p. 3.

altering the size of the dots: ♩ ♩ ♩ ♩ ♩ ♩ ♩ ♩ ♩ ♩ ♩ ♩
Instead, dynamic changes are incorporated in a separate
set of ancillary symbols < > *cresc., mf, ff,* et cetera)
placed above or below the primary symbols, the dots.
Any music instructor knows that all too frequently a
student can keep his eyes only on the primary symbols,
those indicating pitch and length. It is difficult for his
eyes to shift from the dots to the crescendo signs and
back to the dots again.

Bar Lines. The erection of a perpendicular barrier
across the line of progress tends unconsciously to interpret motion. Granted that many musicians learn to over-
look them—or rather to look *through* them—there are
many more who are kept from seeing the unity of the
phrase by its intersection into several compartments. It
is for this reason that we find numerous words of advice
about attitudes toward bar lines. Hans David wrote,
"The proper performance of polyphonic music requires
the ability to visualize melodic lines without regard to
bars." [17] Kennedy-Fraser said, "Indeed, except for the
time-division, try, in reading *all* notation, to *forget the
bars.*" [18] The early Calvinist psalters, instead of bar
lines, had just a small sign on one of the staff lines:

Psalm 107

With these psychological hazards in our present notational system, it might help choral directors to transmute
imaginatively the notation of dots into a notation of lines

[17] *Op. cit.,* p. 7.
[18] *Op. cit.,* p. 7. Used by permission of Paterson's Publications,
Ltd., and Carl Fischer, Inc.

whose relative height represents pitch, whose length signifies duration, whose thickness represents the volume, and whose color indicates quality. Imagine every phrase of isolated notes as an undulating line changing in elevation, shape, and color; yet vibrant, beautiful, intense, or serene. Thus, for example, the folk melody *Picardy* instead of looking like this:

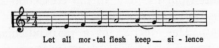

Let all mor-tal flesh keep— si - lence

would appear something like this:

Such a vivid and exact conception of the shape, size, length, and quality of this tone would mean that a choral conductor would much more readily secure the effect he desired as he stood before his chorus. As Scherchen says, "To conduct means to make manifest—without flaws— that which one has perfectly heard within oneself. The sounds must be commanded, and to conduct is to give them shape." [19]

This then is musical expression. Percy Scholes aptly stated it: "Expression in performance is, we might almost say, the name for that part of the music which the composer was not able to commit to writing and which the performer must therefore supply out of his own musical sense and his emotion." [20]

[19] *Op. cit.*, p. 3.
[20] *Op. cit.* Article on expression, p. 301. Used by permission.

CHAPTER V

Conducting—Manifesting the Music to the Singers

First of all, we should recognize that the best choral singing comes from a choir which possesses not only a director whose conducting gestures are eloquent, but also which has a group of singers who are craftsmen in basic choral techniques. No amount of suavity and authority in conducting manners can make up for deficiency in note reading, articulation skill, production of pleasing tone, and phrase shaping. Especially is this individual initiative and skill needed when the director is also involved in playing an organ. Percy Scholes, writing in this connection, used this analogy, "Conducting is generalship on the battlefield of music." [1] Continuing this analogy, we all know that battles are won not only by good strategy at the command posts but also when the line troops know how to use their weapons with deadly effectiveness, how to seek proper shelter, and are acquainted with the many other arts of warfare.

Let us now consider several basic propositions.

1. *Conducting is essential for superior choral singing.* There have been experiments with conductorless orchestras, but the seasoned experience of the major choral and instrumental ensembles across the world is that one person must know and indicate where the music is going and how it is to get there. Even the humblest village

[1] *The Oxford Companion to Music*, p. 217. Used by permission.

choir should have one person in charge of its music making. Although choral conducting could mean any kind of guidance for choirs, here we mean the attention given by a leader who, standing or sitting in view of the choir, indicates by gestures of hands and movements of his body the many interpretative changes in the course of the music.

At this point we should mention a valid, useful, and frequently heard distinction—that a successful choirmaster is not only an able conductor, but also a clever choir trainer. In rehearsal a director is a drillmaster. His manner can be less formal, more spontaneous. He uses much more extreme measures to impress the musical meaning on the singers. Pronounced—even violent—gestures, snapping fingers, clapping hands, occasional patting or stamping feet in time, are employed. He cajoles and instructs while his choir is singing. He does not hesitate to stop them if necessary. He illustrates his desires by singing a snatch of melody. His aim is to fix in his choristers' muscular memory the exact execution of the phrases. Then in performance on Sunday morning he weaves these separate strands in a viable and plastic tapestry of sound. Here his motions are more formal, restrained, but equally intent on creating a "new song unto the Lord."

2. *Able conducting presupposes a clear inner conception of the music.* The most basic requirement for a conductor is the necessity of an exact idea of how the music should sound. The entire preceding chapter on choral music notation was written to make this clear. One of the highest delights for Toscanini was to prop himself up in bed with a stack of symphonic scores on the bedside table. Then, with myopic vision, the great maestro would pore over his beloved Beethoven and regale his

mind with the sounds as Beethoven himself heard them before committing them to paper. Small wonder that Toscanini could evoke heavenly music from his orchestral players. He manifested the music with authority.

A beginner at conducting, however, finds difficulty in looking at an anthem for the first time and transmuting the printed symbols into inner audition. Even playing the accompaniment and parts on the piano are insufficient for complete comprehension. One reliable method is to listen over and over to a good recording of a choral composition with score in hand. If, for example, you plan to use Gustav Holst's setting of "Let all mortal flesh keep silence" (Galaxy #5), purchase or borrow the Mormon Tabernacle Choir recording "The Holly and the Ivy" (Columbia ML 5592), and hear this music repeatedly. Then, without the recording, read mentally through the score. You will find that your inner audition of the finished music comes clearer. As you master the conducting gestures, put the record on and try conducting an imaginary chorus, using five chairs appropriately located to indicate the four sections of singers and the accompanist. Let yourself go. Lose yourself in the music. Then do the same in front of a full-length mirror. Don't be discouraged with what you see the first time. Keep at it.

3. *Conducting should follow conventional procedure and patterns.* Conducting is complete expression of the music. It is foolish to expect the right hand to accomplish this tremendous task. The entire person—body, mind, and spirit—is involved in this manifestation. The graceful movement of arms, hands, and fingers; the strength and mobility of stance; the carriage of body and head; the expressiveness of countenance especially—all these must be involved in conveying the emotions of the music, the shapes of the melodic contours, the tempos,

the relative harmonic intensities, the behavior of the rhythms. One has only to watch Leonard Bernstein face-to-face on a television screen, or to observe topflight choral conductors like Elaine Brown and Robert Shaw, to understand this totality of musical expression.

There are a few conducting gestures which have come to be accepted as conventional throughout the civilized world. In barest form they are designed to indicate the temporal progress of the music. Since music is a time art, one of the main points of reference as the music progresses is the periodic recurrence of a pulsation of time. These beats must be signaled to the musicians in order that simultaneous progress may be made. For centuries these pulsations have been grouped in units of two, three, four, or more beats, and there are gestural patterns to show each set.

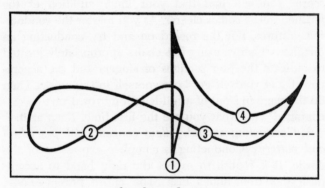

four-beat: legato

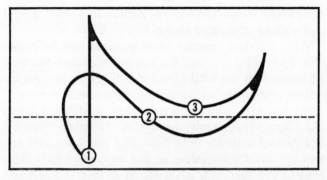

three-beat: legato

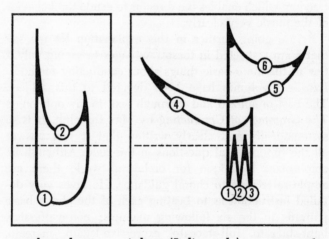

two-beat: legato   six-beat (Italian style): non-expressive

It is extremely important that these standard gestures be mastered by the conductor. While it is possible for members of a particular church choir to accustom themselves to the idiosyncracies of their own director, there is considerable likelihood that this conductor would be

41

completely misunderstood by singers in a joint choral undertaking with other choirs.

With sufficient practice these patterns will be reproduced automatically and the conductor's mind can then be focused on the total job of choral leadership. An excellent routine for anchoring these patterns is a form of eurhythmics in which the conductor, studying a hymn like "Holy, Holy, Holy, Lord God Almighty," beats a 4/4 pattern with his right hand and simultaneously tiptoes the exact time values of the soprano melody. This kind of practice with a variety of hymns and anthems will develop a metrical responsiveness and rhythmical freedom which enables the director to exude the behavior of the music very clearly.

Before going further in this explanation let me say that I am restricted in these few pages to saying only a few of the more basic things about conducting methods. Excellent volumes have been devoted to this subject. The best organized and thorough text, in my opinion, is *The Grammar of Conducting* by Max Rudolph. It is so systematically and clearly written that it will answer all the fundamental questions in this field. Although he emphasizes technique for orchestral work, there are ample references to choral guidance. He gives very detailed instruction as to beating each of the above basic patterns in the six following manners: non-expressive, light-staccato, full-staccato, expressive-legato, marcato, the tenuto. Borrow this book from the library or, better still, buy it, and digest it thoroughly.

The elementary things indicated by conducting gestures are the start, the tempo or motion of the music, and the stop, plus holds and interruptions.

Attack. The conductor gives one extra beat, strictly in tempo, before the music begins. During this preliminary beat the conductor and the choristers breathe rhythmically. The size and intensity of this preliminary sign are governed by the mood and volume of the music.

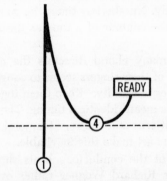

Diagram of preparatory beat for a four-beat measure with music to begin on first count.

Release. The sign for concluding a phrase or section of a piece is clearly shown by a motion of the hand which is usually reinforced by indications with arms, head, and body as needed. The size usually depends on the intensity of tone and emotion at this point. Always there should be some preparatory sign showing that the release is about to occur.

During the motion of the music, the conductor not only concerns himself with the four elements of music— pitch, time, volume, and quality—but he also controls, to some extent at least, word formation as well.

Pitch. Most of the pitch control is established in rehearsal by teaching the right notes. Accuracy of interval leaps, elimination of slurring, good intonation of chords —these are inculcated in the singers. Even so, in actual

43

performance I have seen many conductors give a subtle sign to insure a clean attack in the middle of a pitch, or point a finger upward as the tenors sing a final major third, or raise eyebrows to indicate loftiness on a certain flight of melody. Numberless times the conductor's hand will indicate the contour of a tune as the singers follow it.

Time. For many choral directors the control of the time reactions of their singers seems to constitute the conductor's sole responsibility. "Keep them together" is their motto, and this means identical timing. The nature of the conducting patterns and the very temporal foundation of music as a time art make this inevitable.

The speed of the conductor's beats shows the pace. The composer Richard Wagner rather overemphasized this responsibility for pace control when he wrote: "The whole duty of a conductor is comprised in his ability to indicate the right *tempo*. His choice of *tempi* will show whether he understands the piece or not." [2]

Volume. The conductor's desire for more volume can be indicated by gradually increasing size of gestures, by beckoning motions of the left hand, by more animation in hands and face, and by raised chest. Diminuendos can be shown by lowering the palm of the left hand toward the choir, by finger to lips, by smaller sweeps of the right hand, and by facial expression indicating quietness.

Quality. One of the prime concerns of a conductor is the cultivation of beautiful tone. In rehearsal a choral leader can influence tone markedly. He can effect changes of timbre by calling attention to the necessity of

[2] Richard Wagner, *On Conducting,* translated by Edward Dannreuther (London: W. Reeves, 1897).

good posture, by illustrating with his own voice good and bad sounds, by emphasizing purity of vowel tone, by urging singers to know the limits of volume beyond which strained tone will result.

In final performance the conductor exerts an indirect but profound influence on tonal quality by his skillful portrayal of the mood of the music and especially by his ability to control the breathing of his singers. When choristers yield to the spell of the music their tone will be suffused with many subtle variations of quality just as the moods of a stained-glass window change as the various lights of the day play upon it.

Conducting patterns should be clear but economical. The size of the choral group will determine to some extent the general dimensions of the gestures. A large festival choir of several hundred voices, for example, will require bigger movements than a small group of a dozen voices. It should be apparent, however, that size of gesture alone does not determine clarity. The shape and precision of the patterns contribute much to the ease of communication.

The conductor should strive to eliminate all movements of hands, face, or body which do not contribute to the musical effect. In other words, his conducting should be as simple as possible. There is much thrashing of the air that is entirely uncalled for. It is especially important that church choir directors, in full view of the congregation, should strive for elimination of extraneous motion. As a rule, try to keep the patterns in an imaginary box, less than a foot square, in front of the body.

CHAPTER VI

The Choral Instrument
—The Human Voice

A good choral director should have an adequate knowledge of the structure and mechanics of the human voice, because the voice is the principal instrument upon which he plays. It is generally accepted that a good symphonic conductor should understand the capabilities of the various orchestral instruments as to range, dynamic levels, and quality variation. Such intimate acquaintance-ship enables him to explore more fully the meaning of an orchestral score. If this detailed knowledge of many instruments is expected of a symphonic leader, a choral director may be expected to understand thoroughly the one instrument of his singers—the voice.

The human voice, being a living instrument *within* the singers themselves, is susceptible of amazing develop-ment or tragic abuse, whereas the orchestral instrument comes to the hands of the player a completed work of craftsmanship with its tone quality already fixed. The skillful choir trainer then can accomplish much as he assiduously and expertly molds the unfinished instru-ments of his singers. Such considerations led the Ameri-can Academy of Teachers of Singing to declare:

We believe that the director of a choral group should know the technic of voice. No dean of music or school principal would think of putting a choral conductor in charge of the training of an orchestra or band, but it is a common practice to place the choruses under the direction of a band leader, orchestra conductor, organist or pianist who has no technical knowledge of the voice.[1]

In other words, every choral director can influence the vocal habits of his singers. Whether he models a melodic phrase with a full resonant tone or a tight raucous one, he is conveying specific tonal ideals to his singers just as surely as an art teacher develops color perceptions in his class by his oil sketches on a canvas. His gestures for choral attack repeatedly influence the ease or rigidity of the choristers' breathing. His demands in the higher and lower dynamic levels may cause tension in the larynx and may lead to laryngeal soreness or breathiness.

It is not enough that a voice teacher have factual information regarding the human voice. He must have had some actual experience and training in the proper use of his own voice. Not only is considerable experience as a singer in good choirs helpful, but it is wise also to study voice privately with a skillful teacher.

An extensive anatomical study of the vocal instrument is unnecessary for most choral leaders. However, a basic sketch of the essential parts and functions is invaluable in instilling correct singing habits and in correcting faults.

The Structure of the Vocal Instrument

In the family of musical instruments the human voice is classified as a wind instrument. The basic problems in any wind instrument are, first, to furnish a supply of

[1] *Some Principles in the Care and Development of the Human Voice from Childhood Through Adolescence to Maturity.* From a pronouncement published by the Academy in 1938 and used with their permission. It may be secured through Mr. Harold C. Luckstone, Secretary, 57 Winter Street, Forest Hills 75, New York.

wind, and to set this air in motion along a desired channel; second, to convert this stream of air into a series of vibrations; and, third, to amplify and modify this stream of vibrations.

A study of the anatomy of the human body discloses that the vocal instrument possesses equipment for doing all three of these things. This is clearly shown in the following diagram. Alongside it is placed a diagram of an organ pipe of the reed family. This type of pipe illustrates the structure of the human voice.

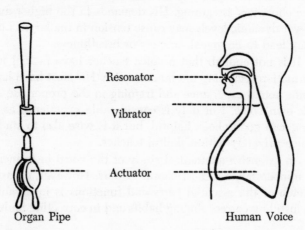

Resonator

Vibrator

Actuator

Organ Pipe   Human Voice

Organ Pipe

1. Actuator: The bellows or in most modern organs the electric blower.

2. Vibrator: The metal strip or reed which flutters against the opening of the shallot.

3. Resonator: The metal cylinder above the reed which occupies most of the length of the pipe.

Human Voice

1. Actuator: The lungs acted upon by ribs and diaphragm.

2. Vibrator: The vocal folds in the larynx.

3. Resonator: The cavities of throat, nose, and mouth.

48

Breathing

Skill in breathing is necessary in artistic singing. The sustaining of long phrases, changes in dynamics, quietness of inhalation, and clarity of vocal tone are related to breathing, and are essential for beautiful, expressive singing.

Air is set in motion by some pressure against it. One of the simplest means is by waving a fan. The fan, however, presses air in many directions. Centuries ago men became aware of the need for a focused stream of air; in making a fire, for example, man needed a means of directing a steady stream of air on a single glowing ember. He took two fans and connected them by a flexible leather membrane, thus making a simple bellows. The inward movement of the two solid, fan-like sides created pressure on the air and forced it to seek an outlet. This emission of air might be called *expiration*.

When the handles of the bellows are drawn away from each other pressure within is reduced and a partial vacuum is created. Outside atmospheric pressure forces air back into the interior. This inward motion might be called *inspiration*. With this introductory analogy in mind, we shall consider the human respiratory apparatus. It consists basically of two parts: (1) The lungs, and (2) muscles and bones which exert pressures upon the lungs causing air to flow in and out of them.

1. The lungs are sponge-like, pear-shaped organs located on each side of the chest cavity. Each may be compared to a tree which has a direct channel connection between the main trunk and each individual leaf by means of larger limbs, smaller branches, and minute twigs. Nature has not provided within the lung structure

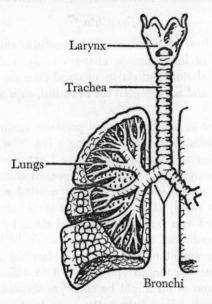

Larynx

Trachea

Lungs

Bronchi

itself any means of changing its size or shape. Therefore, the means of changing pressure, necessary for setting air in motion, must be sought elsewhere.

2. Nature has provided two sets of forces to act upon the lungs—an in-and-out pressure and an up-and-down pressure. The in-and-out pressure is provided by movement of the ribs, which acts upon the lungs much as the two solid sides of the bellows act to produce expiration and inspiration. A glance at the diagram will show that the ribs are laced together with intercostal muscles, which not only form a tight wall for retaining the vital organs but also act as a lifting agent for the ribs. As these muscles contract, the ribs are drawn up and out and so enlarge the space containing the lungs.

50

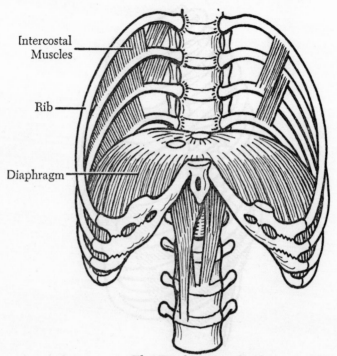

Intercostal Muscles

Rib

Diaphragm

The Diaphragm and Ribs

The up-and-down pressure is provided by the action of the diaphragm which is a group of large muscles and sinews serving as the partition between the thoracic and abdominal cavities. This muscle is normally dome shaped and fits snugly against the bottom of both lungs. When this large muscle contracts it flattens, drawing the lungs downward and causing them to expand in capacity. This is *inhalation*. The return movement of the diaphragm upwards is assisted by the contraction of the wall of the abdominal muscles and by the inward recoil of the rib-cage

51

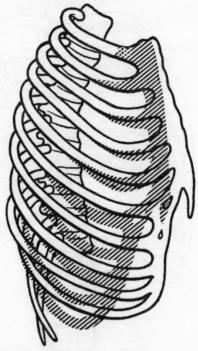

This figure shows increase in the dimensions of the chest when the ribs are elevated in inhalation. The shaded portion represents the thorax after exhalation; the clear portion after the ribs have been raised at the end of inhalation. A side view would show similar spread laterally at end of inhalation.

which gives additional thrust to the upward action. This outward movement of the air is called *exhalation.*

This method of breathing is favored by the American Academy of Teachers of Singing. In *An Outline of Theory* they summarized their beliefs about breathing:

1. Believes in teaching the pupil how to breathe.

2. Believes that the correct practice of singing in itself tends to develop and establish the mastery of the breath.

3. Believes that the singer should stand comfortably erect, with the chest medium high, and with a feeling of flexibility and well-being.

4. Favors that method of breathing which is known scientifically as "Diaphragmatic-Costal," colloquially as "deep breathing."

5. Believes that, in inhalation the upper abdomen expands, owing to the descent of the diaphragm, and the ribs expand; in exhalation the abdomen tenses and contracts, owing to the pressure of the abdominal muscles and to the gradual ascent of the diaphragm, and ribs contract. Thus the greatest observable effect in both inhalation and exhalation is in front and at the sides in the region of the waist-line.

6. Believes that either the mouth or the nose may be used in inhalation.

7. Recommends the daily practice of calisthenics or setting-up exercises.[2]

Tone Production

The actual vocal tone is produced in the larynx. This organ, the "voice-box," is a complicated mechanism whose description in detail is quite unnecessary. Suffice

[2] *An Outline of Theory,* adopted by the American Academy of Teachers of Singing for their individual guidance, December 9, 1925, and used by permission.

it to say that it contains horizontal folds or bands which are called vocal cords. These folds move rapidly toward and away from each other in a kind of rolling motion. They act somewhat like the human lips when a trumpet is placed against them and a trumpeter's lips vibrate to produce a tone.

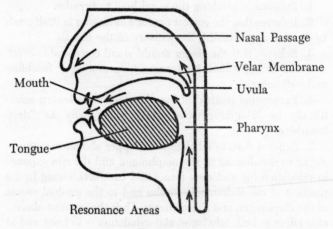

Resonance

The vocal tones which leave the larynx are comprised of complicated streams of vibrations. These sounds are acted upon mainly by the cavities of the head. The diagram to the left shows three principal resonance areas: (1) The pharynx is the large tube-like area in the back of the throat which acts mainly to enlarge the sound. (2) The nasal passages are used especially in the production of consonant sounds of *m*, *n*, and *ng*. (3) The oral cavity is most important because of its mobility. The tongue is the main flexibility factor. Words are a product mainly of this resonance area of the vocal mechanism. This subject is considered in the next chapter.

54

The American Academy of Teachers of Singing has given a concise and sound summary of this subject.

Tone. Good vocal tone depends upon a concept of beautiful sound and upon a sensitive and educated ear.

It results from the consequent co-ordination of the following:

1. Controlled breath;

2. A larynx whose normal position, neither locally raised nor lowered, is insured by correct inhalation, and allows freedom of action of the tongue to which it is attached;

3. Vocal cords in unhindered vibration.

These three produce a fundamental tone, proportionately reinforced by

4. The resonance chambers of the chest and the head (mouth and nasal cavities) and issuing through

5. A free throat;

6. Tongue, palate, lips, and jaw, all freely active in pronouncing, without rigidity, and with no locally specialized effort for supposed aid to the tone.

This tone, easy flowing, smooth, permits and favors every variety of expression in singing. Its inception, following inhalation, is the Attack; that is, the immediate application of breath to the vocal cords, after pitch and vowel adjustment of the whole vocal apparatus.[3]

For further information regarding the structure and use of the human voice see William Rice's *Basic Principles of Singing,* and the article on "Voice Training" in *Grove's Dictionary of Music and Musicians.*[4]

[3] *An Outline of Theory.* Adopted April 14, 1926. Used by permission.

[4] Rice (Nashville: Abingdon Press, 1960), and *Grove's Dictionary of Music and Musicians,* edited by Eric Blom (5th ed.; New York: The Macmillan Company, 1954). See Bibliography for additional suggestions.

55

CHAPTER VII

Singing Is Correct
and Beautiful Speech Sustained—
Choral Diction

The cultivated human voice is one of the most beautiful of all musical instruments. This is so not only because the instrument, being within the person, is susceptible of very sensitive control, but also because it is the one instrument which can form words. This ability to convey intellectual conceptions is the unique thing about the human voice. The singer thus can add a content of ideas to the purely aesthetic and emotional quality of the music.

The problem of transmitting this intellectual content to the listeners should be one of the basic concerns of any singer. Sung commercials on the radio must get the "message" over or they are not used. In the church it is singular that congregations week after week will tolerate unintelligibility in a soloist or choir when a preacher would be severely criticized for faulty diction. Possibly one reason for this tolerance is that the music itself speaks a language even without the meaning of the words. It is especially important that singers who have dedicated their talents to making music for the worship of Almighty God should study to be superb craftsmen in this art of clearly sung speech.

This task has been an age-old concern of the Church. The Apostle Paul affirmed, "in the congregation I would rather speak five intelligible words, for the benefit of others as well as myself, than thousands of words in the language of ecstasy." (I Cor. 14:19, New English Bible.) Although he was referring to a special problem in the Corinthian church, where some were speaking in strange tongues of ecstasy, he enunciated a principle which could be evoked in defense of clear diction. Fifteen hundred years later, the reformer John Calvin expressed a similar view when he wrote, "It is also expedient and reasonable that all should know and hear what is said and done in the temple, to receive fruit and edification therefrom." [1]

A few years later in England, Queen Elizabeth decreed even more explicitly "that there be a modest and distinct song so used in all parts of the common prayers in the church, that the same may be as plainly understanded, as if it were read without singing." [2]

Diction for the Individual Singer

The individual singer holds the key to good choral diction. As each choir member improves in diction, to that extent the choir as a whole will develop.

1. *Each singer must have a clear concept of the intellectual and emotional meaning of the text.* The starting point towards craftsmanship in diction is singing with understanding, which means that the individual singer must have a clear conception of the intellectual and emotional meaning of the text. Many choirs know that they can read English, and so they dive right into learning the notes, whereas it is important to determine first what

[1] Foreword to *Geneva Psalter*, 1543. Translation from Oliver Strunk, ed., *Source Readings in Music History* (New York: W. W. Norton & Company, 1950), p. 345.

[2] Gee and Hardy, *Documents Illustrative of English Church History*, p. 435.

is the topic of the text. If there are stanzas, learn what is the theme of each and how they progress in logic toward the climax in the last stanza. Keep in mind to whom the text is addressed, whether to God the Father and Creator, as in the anthem "O God of Love, O King of Peace," or to the congregation in the anthem "O taste and see how gracious the Lord is," or to oneself as in the American folk melody "What wondrous love is this, O my soul." As the Apostle Paul wrote, "I will sing with the spirit, and I will sing with the understanding also." (I Cor. 14:15, K.J.V.)

2. *Each singer should have a crystal-clear conception of the basic sounds of the language and should be able to produce them at will.* Here we move into the realm of the tools and materials of speech. Just as the architect and contractor have bricks, boards, cement, and nails for use in constructing a house, so a singer has small bits of sound, distinct from one another, which can be assembled in various combinations to make words. These basic units of the English language are called *speech sounds*. They are divided into three classes—vowels, diphthongs, and consonants. With severe space limitations, we can give only an introduction to this extensive subject.

A. *Vowels.* Grant Fairbanks, a speech authority, has said: "A vowel is a voiced speech sound in which the vocal cord tone is selectively modified as it passes through the resonance cavities of the throat and head. . . . Different vowels are produced by changing the characteristics of the cavities, and probably the most important factor in this process is the variation of tongue position." [3]

[3] *Voice and Articulation Drillbook* (New York: Harper & Brothers, 1940), p. 21.

58

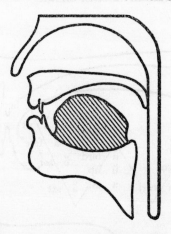

In the diagram we see a side view of the mouth cavity showing the nasal passage at the top, the nose and lips at the left, and the tongue in the mouth cavity. You will notice that the tongue is lifted high toward the front of the mouth and is in the formation to produce the vowel *ē* as in the word "beet."

Perhaps the quickest way to comprehend the function of the tongue in forming clear vowels is to study the following diagram which shows the major vowel colors of the English language.

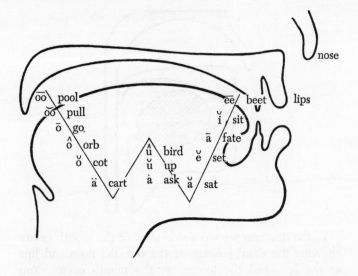

Here we see the W-shaped vowel spectrum located over an elongated drawing of the mouth cavity. On the right hand you see the front vowels, in the center three middle vowels, with the back vowels in the slanting column at the left. It will be helpful if the reader will pronounce each vowel sound with its key word and observe how the front, middle, or back of the tongue rises or descends as the series of sounds are made. It should be emphasized that this diagram is purely schematic and does not purport to give exact tongue locations. It should be helpful, though, in giving some notion of relative positions of the tongue as well as its direction of movement. For further detailed, authoritative, and readily available information on these tongue positions see the essay on pronunciation in *Webster's New International Dictionary* (G. & C. Merriam Co.), second edition, unabridged, Section 31 on front, central, and back vowels. The entire essay is valuable reading for information on any of the sounds briefly described in this chapter.

William Shakespeare, a famous teacher of singing—not the playwright, constructed a clever sentence which, when pronounced, causes your tongue to pass through each of the stations of the vowel spectrum we have just outlined, starting with the high back vowels and ending in the high front position: "Who would know aught of art must learn and then take his ease." [4]

It is essential that a singer learn to position his tongue so that each separate vowel is clearly formed. There is a special danger of ambiguity between vowels that are produced by adjacent locations of the tongue such as "wuhship" instead of "worship," "git" instead of "get," and "ruhm" instead of "room."

B. *Diphthongs.* A diphthong is comprised of two vowel sounds changing from one to the other in one syllable. There are four diphthongs in the English language:

$\bar{\imath}$ as in "ice"   composed of $\ddot{a}$ (arm) plus $\breve{\imath}$ (sit)

ou as in "out" composed of $\ddot{a}$ (arm) plus $\breve{o}\breve{o}$ (foot)

oi as in "oil" composed of $\hat{o}$ (orb) plus $\breve{\imath}$ (sit)

$\bar{u}$ as in "cube" composed of $\begin{matrix} \breve{\imath} \ (\text{sit}) \\ y \ (\text{yes}) \end{matrix}$ plus $\bar{o}\bar{o}$ (food)

Two additional sounds are sometimes classified as diph-

---

[4] *Plain Words on Singing* (London: G. P. Putnam's Sons, 1924), p. 52. Shakespeare said, concerning the practice of whispering vowels, "When, by assiduous practice, we succeed in correctly tuning these whispers, we have an exact pattern of the shape of the spaces which should form themselves in the mouth and throat during singing." Then he suggested this sentence for memorizing the vowel "spectrum": "Who knows aught of art must learn, and then take his ease." If we substitute "would know" for "knows," we have added an essential vowel.

thongs: $\bar{a}$ ($\check{a}$ plus $\check{i}$) and $\bar{o}$ ($\bar{o}$ plus $\widecheck{oo}$). The singer should be taught a policy of apportioning the proper time to each vowel of the diphthong. He must realize that one of the two vowels is the more important and that it must receive by far the greater proportion of time. Fred Waring suggests, "Give subsidiary vowel and tuned consonant sounds a proportionate, rhythmic amount of the full time value." [5]

In the list of four diphthongs given earlier, the first three have the principal vowel first with the subordinate or vanish vowel second. The fourth diphthong reverses this order.

C. *Consonants.* A consonant is a speech sound which is formed when the expired breath stream is diverted, hindered, or stopped during its emission. This statement will be better understood if we give the following three ways of classifying consonants.

a. *In consonants the breath stream may be the total source of sound or the vowel fold tone may be added to it.* Two consonants formed by identical articulators which use the same action for each—one having only breath stream noise, the other adding to this noise *vocal tone*—are called *cognates.* Pronounce the following list of cognates and you will understand this statement.

[5] *Tone Syllables* (Delaware Water Gap, Pa.: Shawnee Press, 1945), p. 6.

Unvoiced		*Voiced*	
p	pay	*b*	bay
t	to	*d*	do
k	cane	*g*	gain
th	ether	*th*	either
f	fan	*v*	van
s	sink	*z*	zinc
sh	glacier	*zh*	glazier
ch	etch	*j*	edge
hw	white	*w*	wite

b. *A consonant may have the breath stream diverted, hindered, or completely stopped.* The consonants *m, n,* and *ng* are made by *diverting* the breath stream and vocal cord tone through the nasal passages by forming a dam at the lips, at the tip of the tongue, and at the back of the tongue.

The breath stream is *hindered* only slightly in the glide consonants, *w, hw,* and *y,* and in the semi-vowels, *l* and *r.* There is considerable restriction and hindrance when sibilants are produced by forcing air through a small opening—*s, z, f, v, th, th, sh, zh,* and *h.*

In the formation of *p, b, t, d, k,* and *g* the breath stream is completely *stopped* and explosively released; hence their name "stop-plosives."

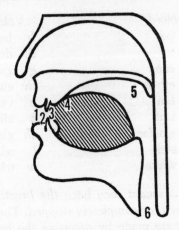

c. *Consonants are classified according to which articulators are used in their formation.*

In the diagram we see the interior of a mouth with articulators such as lips, teeth, tongue, hard and soft palates. Each location is numbered. Singers' diction is improved as they understand how consonants are produced. Lip consonants, (1) *m, hw, w, p,* and *b,* are produced by action of lips. Lip-teeth consonants, (2) *f* and *v,* are formed by interaction of lower lip and teeth. Tongue-teeth consonants (3) *th* and *th,* are made by the tongue and teeth. Post-dental consonants, (4) *n, t, d, r, l, s, z, sh, zh,* and *y,* are formed by the tongue acting against the roof of the mouth just back of the upper teeth. Soft-palate consonants, (5) *ng, k,* and *g,* are shaped by the interaction of the back of the tongue and the soft palate shown at the upper right of the picture. Then, finally, there is the glottal consonant, (6) *h,* which is produced at the opening between the vocal cords or glottis.

Consonants, like choir gowns, must be the right size.

64

Consonants can be too long or too short, too loud or too soft. Just as vowels can be sung with varying degrees of power, so consonants have volume. A singer consequently should be careful to use a consonant volume appropriate to its adjacent vowel. Sibilants and explosives need special care.

Some consonants have pitch, some do not. An unvoiced explosive like *t* does not have pitch. Others like *m* and *l* do, and thus need special consideration in enunciation to prevent slurring from pitch to pitch.

One simple way to sharpen enunciation and to become aware of the sounds is to produce only the vowels in a sentence. Another method of improving speech is to whisper the sentence. This brings into clear focus the manner in which the articulators work in your mouth to form the vowels and consonants.

3. *Each singer should be able to assemble these three basic speech sounds—vowels, diphthongs, and consonants—into words after the patterns of sound and accent set by superior speakers in that country. This is pronunciation.* Noice that both sound and accent must be correct. In the familiar word "extra" the final syllable is frequently mispronounced *ĭ* instead of *uh*. In the word "adúlt" the stress, frequently placed on the first syllable, should be on the second syllable according to most authorities.

A helpful exercise for both director and choristers in developing perception of the separate sounds in words is the dissection of random words. "This means a good lunch," written phonetically, would be: "th ĭ s m ē n z ŭ go͝od lŭnch." A good dictionary is indispensable in checking your analysis. Give your choir practice in ear training by asking them to take a word apart and give you the separate sounds.

4. *Each singer should be able to sing the text with the naturalness of superior connected speech.* At least four problems confront a singer who attempts this. (1) He must give sufficient stress to important words in a phrase. (2) He should handle unaccented syllables with care. (3) He must reconcile the musical phrasing with the text wherever necessary. (4) He must preserve word identity while maintaining strict legato.

Diction for Choruses

We have outlined some of the qualifications for beautiful, clear diction in a single singing voice. We turn now to the problem of combining the diction of many individuals so that a chorus may be as clearly understood as a single singer.

1. *Choristers should use identical vowel colors.* We speak of various vowel *colors.* If you want a gallon of bright red paint and have asked four painters to contribute one quart each to a gallon container, you require that each brings a quart of bright red paint of identical hue. You will get a muddled shade if one quart tends toward brown, another toward orange, and so on. If twenty choristers are sustaining the word "then," we must hear the vowel ĕ as in "set," not ă or *uh* or ĭ.

2. *Choristers should form identical consonants.* There is an accepted standard for every consonant, and if forty people are to communicate this sound each singer must produce an accurately articulated consonant. For example, suppose a choir is completing an anthem with the word "God." The final sound would be the *voiced* explosive *d.* The vocal tone continues *through* the consonant. Suppose half the choir makes it a true voiced *d* and one half stops the voice before the final consonant, mak-

ing the sound *t*. (We will forget for the moment those who sound no final consonant!) The listener might not know whether the intended word was "God" or "got." Connotation might resolve the uncertainty, but singers should strive not to be ambiguous because of carelessly made consonants.

3. *Choristers should produce vowels and consonants simultaneously.* A basic prerequisite for obedience to this rule is an identical strong rhythmic impulse felt by each chorister, so that the choir arrives at and departs from each vowel and consonant simultaneously. In the Preface to *The Church Anthem Book* the editors incorporated this principle in the following simple formula:

Time every consonant
Tone every vowel   } to your team
Tune every note

Before giving a few practical suggestions for procuring better diction, we should state that it is much easier to communicate choral diction in homophonic—chord-like—music rather than in polyphonic—multilinear—music.

Practical Suggestions for Improving Diction

1. Rehearse the choir so well that the singers know the notes perfectly and thus can concern themselves with projecting the thought and emotion.

2. Urge the singers to "speak the words" while singing. Singing is correct and beautiful speech sustained. As Plunkett Greene's *Main Rule III* expressed it, "Sing as you speak." [6]

[6] *Interpretation in Song* (London: Macmillan and Company, 1931), p. 104.

3. Encourage your choristers to sing with exaggerated distinctness.

4. Make a recording of the choir with microphones in front of and above the singers. Then place the microphones halfway back in the church.

5. After the anthem is sufficiently mastered, invite a guest, unacquainted with the particular anthem text, to sit in the back of the rehearsal room or church. After the choir has sung a phrase ask him to repeat the words to the choir. This practice is usually most revealing and helpful to a choir.

6. Divide the choir into two halves, and while one group faces away from the blackboard, have the others read words sounding almost alike from the board, for example, "view," "pew," "stew," or "seat," "meat," "beat." Let those with their backs to the board attempt to repeat the words. Reverse the groups and try the game again.

7. Write the words of the anthem on the blackboard in phonetic spelling.

CHAPTER VIII

Training the Choir
During Rehearsal

One of the most important secrets of a successful choir is beautiful vital music well sung. Choristers and director alike know when they have done a good job. At this moment they share their Creator's satisfaction in a task well performed—"And God saw every thing that he had made, and, behold, it was very good." (Gen. 1:31, K.J.V.). The rehearsers do not have to wait until Sunday morning to encounter God. When, in rehearsal, they give a dotted half note the correct time value they worship him "in truth." God involves himself in the totality of a dedicated life.

Before detailing methods of managing a rehearsal I would like to make several preliminary comments.

Investigators of the learning process have outlined a number of ways whereby persons learn data and techniques, many of which can be used interchangeably by choir trainers. The *project* method is most widely used in rehearsals. In this, an anthem or cantata is mastered by applying a number of basic choral principles in a specific project. The *lecture* method is used hardly at all, although it could have real value. It need not be an hour's discourse on the history of church music or on consonant formation, but a five- or ten-minute elucidation or analysis of how to breathe, on the function of the tongue in enunciation, or on the meaning of phrasing can frequently save hours of rehearsal time later on. The *discussion* method has many implications for an imaginative director. A three-minute discussion on some choral question can start choristers' minds clicking. Questions like these can stimulate discussion: "What is the climax of this phrase?" (playing it over); "What does this text mean— 'And that love may never cease, I will move Thee'?" (From George Herbert's "King of Glory, King of Peace"); or "Do you like this style of music? Why, or why not?" Do not be afraid of difference of opinion. These discussions need not be overdone.

Balance short-term goals of mastering next Sunday's anthems with long-range educational projects. Remember that you are training musicians as well as teaching them blocks of music. Divide the year's rehearsal periods into emphasis units, giving a month or so to concentration on such topics as breathing for singing, tone production, diction (vowels, diphthongs, consonants), the stuff of music, interpretation, styles of music, service manners, et cetera. This long-range planning will keep your program well rounded. Your singers will feel steady growth. These emphases can be inserted into rehearsal periods by explanations of varying lengths, by displaying posters and other exhibits, and by other ingenious means.

The director of the average amateur choir needs unique adaptiveness and understanding. Earlier I used the analogy of the director of an amateur choir being similar to the teacher of a one-room school with grades one through six. The director of a professional choir might be the equivalent of an English professor conducting a seminar on the works of Spencer, the English poet. This professor knows that his students already have had a background in English literature. There are directors, like Fred Waring, whose professional singers must pass formidable music reading tests, must have impeccable tone quality, and must be able to shape any consonant with the skill of a lapidary. The prerequisites for membership in his glee club are clearly demarked and rigidly adhered to.

An amateur choir frequently has no entrance requirements. Directors of such choirs may have beginners who are unsure of their ability to carry a melody, much less to stay on the bass or alto track. Others in this same choir may have extensive choir experience and a wide musical vocabulary. Some are musical illiterates, others agile readers. This disparity of levels of knowledge and skill need not discourage the clever director. He will enlist the help of the abler singers as section leaders—having them sit in back where their voices can influence, but not scream into, the others.

While we are discussing section leaders, Margaret Kuhn, prominent social psychologist, wrote in this regard:

To be the formal leader of any group is no simple assignment. No one person could possibly succeed in it alone, without the presence and interaction of informal leaders, and the response and support of group members, and the guidance of the Holy Spirit.

Although students of group life can identify many roles which informal leaders may take in groups, we briefly summarize only two rather broad functions which are fulfilled to some extent in every group:

1. In every group informal leaders develop and maintain group spirit and morale, and help to create cohesiveness, so that members feel a sense of fellowship and "we-ness," and take pride and satisfaction in being identified with the group. When there is conflict, for example, these *social leaders* keep up the morale of the group-as-a-whole, by a joke that relieves tension and gets a laugh, or by a

71

compliment that calms ruffled feelings. They show great
sensitivity to individual needs and emotions.

2. Informal leaders also assume *task leader* roles, and help
to keep the group-as-a-whole on the ball. . . .[1]

The director should preserve a realistic, common-sense
approach to the whole rehearsal problem. Be encouraging. Realize that legitimate compliments create confidence. Recognize that your singers want to do a good job
but may not have been trained in many of the basic techniques. It would be stupid for the master furniture maker
to chide his new apprentice for bringing him an awl instead of a chisel if the lad had not first been taught the
distinction between the various kinds of woodworking
tools. So a chorus master need not be furious at a section
for not holding a whole note four beats when they have
not been taught how to feel the four pulses. Nor need
he be irked at their dropping final consonants if they
have not had consonantal drills. Remember that all par-
ticipants in rehearsal endeavor, director and choristers
alike, have limitations.

Now we get down to practical suggestions. The following eighteen items are divided into three groupings—
things to be attended to before, during, and after rehearsals.

Before Rehearsal

1. *Plan exactly what is to be accomplished in each rehearsal, and, as a rule, write down the plan in detail.*
Most rehearsals are planned to some extent. Unless a

[1] Quoted from *You Can't Be Human Alone.* Published by The
National Council of Churches. Copyright 1956. Used with permission. P. 10.

carefully thought out strategy is followed, however, unbalanced practices are apt to result. Too much time, for example, will be spent on one anthem and too little on the rest. Sometimes there is so much dawdling for several weeks that eventually there is a mad scramble to get an anthem ready for Sunday.

In planning each practice, realize that you cannot do three hours' work in two. I have witnessed—and conducted—tense, frantic rehearsals in which the director tried to cover too much territory. Poise and fresh eagerness come with careful planning.

In preparing for a rehearsal keep these things in mind: The exact order of the musical numbers to be rehearsed, whether or not the starting anthem is relatively familiar, subtle details in frequently sung responses or liturgical music which require improvement, whether any unfamiliar hymn tunes are to be used in the next service, the plans for the next five or more weeks, when the announcements are to be made, and the necessity for a brief period of relaxation in a long rehearsal. Incidentally, these intermissions are very useful in developing fellowship and in supplying a chance to catch up on the news. These and other matters should be outlined and not left to chance.

A beginning director especially should have a written rehearsal design on the conductor's stand or piano rack. This—and a large wall clock in front of him—will do much to keep things moving smoothly. Some deviation and spontaneity is to be expected, but the basic itinerary is a steadying influence.

2. *Absorb the music thoroughly before trying to teach it.* The better the director knows the music, the sooner and the better the choir will sing it. I cannot overemphasize that the image of the music must be imprinted on the mind of the director.

73

The text of the anthem should be pondered and read aloud. The music should be studied, sung, and played over and over until the harmonies are mastered, the different voice parts learned, and the rhythmic patterns responded to. Note carefully the composer's or editor's tempos or dynamic markings. You owe it to him to try them. If you strongly disagree substitute your own indications. After all, the composer may have had in mind an enormous reverberant cathedral, whereas your church may have a small, "dry," acoustically dead interior. Ralph Vaughan Williams, for example, marked ♩=60 at the beginning of his anthem "O how amiable." As a rule, I have found it necessary to take it at about eighty beats per minute. As Percy Young advises, "We should regard the music in relation to the building in which it is performed and adjust *tempi* accordingly." [2]

The difficult spots in the anthem should be isolated and analyzed to determine why they are stumbling blocks and which voice is most apt to err. In the director's copy these danger points should be circled with a colored pencil. In the choral sections of the anthem the prominent melody should be underlined, particularly when it lies in the lower voice parts, as a reminder that this part may need highlighting. Breathing spots should be noted by an apostrophe. Analysis of the form of the anthem will lead to discovery of the principal climax and subordinate peaks and to identification of repeat sections. It is a great help if the anthem can be memorized.

Such study will give the director confidence and freedom when he is before the choir. A choir can give only what the director expects and asks for.

[2] *The Choral Tradition* (London: Hutchinson & Company, Ltd., 1962), p. 12.

3. *Come to rehearsal prepared for strenuous work.* The conductor should come to rehearsal ready to elicit all he can from the singers. Church choir singers bring to rehearsal the accumulation of the day's fatigue, and they need to be lifted out of this. This takes a great deal of physical and psychic energy. If possible plan the prior activities of the rehearsal day so that an ample reserve is stored for expenditure in the practice room. A visit to a rehearsal conducted by Ifor Jones of the Bach Bethlehem Choir, Elaine Brown of Philadelphia, or Robert Shaw of Cleveland will quickly convince the neophyte that vital rehearsals are the outcome of an enormous reservoir of energy.

4. *See that the rehearsal room is efficiently arranged.* The orderliness and efficiency of the room will be reflected in the precision and command of the singing. This is discussed in some detail in *Planning for Church Music.*[3] Some items to be considered are non-drafty, adequate ventilation, sufficient illumination, acoustics neither too dead nor too reverberant, tasteful interior decoration, posture-supporting chairs arranged uncrowdedly so that the director can move easily among singers. The piano should be either grand or studio-size so pianist can look over at singers. A large wall clock located in view of director and behind singers is absolutely necessary. Filing cabinets for anthem storage should be handy to the director. Install a bulletin board near the doorway for display of notices, anthem lists, and cartoons. A table conveniently located can hold the music stacks for the rehearsal or, if folders are used, they can be stored in racks with vertical partitions. Church music magazines and textbooks should be available.

[3] Sydnor, *op. cit.* See Ch. IV, "The Rehearsal Room."

5. *Use an orderly, time-saving method of distributing music.* Rehearsal time is valuable time. Many precious minutes are lost while five or ten anthems are issued and collected before and after each number is sung. Some directors place stacks of the current anthems near the door, where each singer collects and deposits a copy of each before and after rehearsal. Other directors prefer that each singer get the same copy at each rehearsal in order that any penciled notations made the previous week may be available, in which case the anthems are kept in sets assigned to each singer and are stored in a folder or notebook.

6. *A definite seating plan should be followed.* Directors frequently find it wise, as a rule, to arrange practice room chairs in the approximate formation found in the loft or chancel. Thus the singers hear the relationships of voices and sounds encountered in the performance situation. It will increase interest, musicianship, and self-reliance, however, if flexible plans are followed. Men's sections are usually seated behind the women's sections, tenors behind altos, basses behind sopranos, or the reverse. Try putting the men in front during part of the rehearsal or behind the opposite section from the usual arrangement. Sometimes ask the choir to stand in compact formation around the piano. On other occasions leave enough room to walk between rows of singers. If you have enough singers, and if the anthem is well learned, divide the choir into two fairly well-balanced choral groups. The singers can thus hear each other and the other parts better than when they are enmeshed in the middle of singers of similar voice. Then pair the singers—two tenors, two altos, et cetera—and run through the music. Finally, arrange the group as quartets and have them sing

the music. Done tactfully, this is a fine tonic for intonation and blending.

During Rehearsal

7. *Begin on time. "Well begun is half done."* One reason many singers are late at rehearsals may be that the beginning of rehearsal is neither on schedule nor significant. First of all, make a point of starting on time regardless of the number present. In a nice but positive manner let the choir know that you are extremely conscious of time and its value in rehearsal. To warm up the voices some directors begin by singing straight through a well-known anthem which is not too demanding vocally. Others use loosening-up exercises—scales and chords sung on various pitches with different vowel and consonant combinations, attacks, releases, crescendi and dimuendi. Not only does this make the vocal mechanism supple but it also brings the attention of the singers to a close focus on the director. Vary the exercises occasionally to give fresh interest, and explain the value of each particular exercise.

After this vigorous initiation, work may then be started immediately, while attention is keenest, on the most difficult music of the evening.

8. *Except in most unusual circumstances, rehearse an anthem at least four or five weeks before using it in church service.* I cannot overemphasize this suggestion. Repetition is one of the fundamental laws of learning. One of a choirmaster's joys is to bring a choir to a Sunday service with the confident knowledge that the anthem is bound to "go." It takes time to reach this state. Let the goal be "the unashamed chorister."

One of the major complaints about many choral directors is that they do not allow singers sufficient time to learn the music. Singers—especially amateurs—find it embarrassing to be asked to perform insufficiently practiced music. Even if you cannot get the sermon or service topics in time, work out your schedule weeks in advance. Follow the church year. That is fixed and known. Later, when your choir has a more extensive repertoire, you can dip into the file to find an anthem appropriate to a service several weeks off and bring it back to fine polish in a shorter time.

9. *The director should balance judiciously the detailed study of short difficult spots with uninterrupted singing of long sections of anthems.* Some conductors have their singers read through an anthem several times and hope that it is learned. This reminds one of Philipp Spitta's description of Robert Schumann's rehearsal fiascos:

Any thorough practice bit by bit with his orchestra, with instructive remarks by the way as to the mode of execution, was impossible to this great artist, who in this respect was a striking contrast to Mendelssohn. He would have a piece played through, and if it did not answer to his wishes, had it repeated. If it went no better the second, or perhaps even a third time, he would be extremely angry at what he considered the clumsiness or even the ill-will of the players; but detailed remarks he never made.[4]

Other directors move phrase by phrase through the pages looking for flaws, then diligently correcting them. Exclusive use of the first method is dangerous in that it leaves unremoved many potential stumbling blocks. Too much of the second method is apt to yield a disjunct,

[4] Article on Robert Schumann in *Grove's Dictionary of Music and Musicians.*

78

labored composition in final performance, and, as Sir Adrian Boult wrote, "Nothing is more irritating to players and singers than continual stoppages, and the strain can be compared to that caused to a delicate engine." [5]

The foundation of good singing is accuracy. Speaking of conducting, Vaughan Williams wrote, "Up to the middle of the 19th century a fairly correct performance was all that a conductor expected of his players: now correctness is the minimum from which he starts." [6] Or, as Marjory Kennedy-Fraser expresses it, "We must live under the law before we can live under grace!" [7]

When first singing a new number it is helpful to run through the anthem several times without stopping, regardless of stumbling. One of these excursions might profitably be done slowly. Next, give attention to mastering any difficult spots, transforming the weakest passages into the strongest ones. Charles Cooke has a true analogy when he compares this process to setting a fractured bone. "Surgeons tell us," he wrote, "that a broken arm or leg, if it is correctly set, becomes strongest at the point of the fracture." [8] I have a conductor friend who makes it a habit to have his choir repeat correctly three times any spot that has been "fractured." This anchors the correct procedure in the muscular memories and reflexes of the singers.

When a person conducts a choir he is simultaneously

[5] *A Handbook on the Technique of Conducting* (7th ed.; Oxford: Hall the Printer, Limited, 1949), p. 39.

[6] Article on conducting in *Grove's Dictionary of Music and Musicians.*

[7] *Hebridean Song and the Laws of Interpretation,* p. 14. Used by permission of Paterson's Publications, Ltd., and Carl Fischer, Inc.

[8] *Playing the Piano for Pleasure* (New York: Simon & Schuster, Inc., 1960), p. 49.

involved and detached. Unlike the football coach who directs his team from the sideline bench, the director is "in the game." Yet he is at the same time a diagnostician. As the choir progresses through the singing of an anthem he should follow Sir Adrian Boult's advice and make a mental checklist of things which need correcting and simultaneously begin arranging them in order of greater or lesser importance. When the choir stops singing, the conductor may have ten comments to make, but, in the interest of efficiency and with respect for human memory, he may explain only some of his complaints. He should note which are mere slips and which are radical and need correcting.

After the "fractures" have been set and the rough places made smooth, then the consecutive feeling for the music must be restored by unimpeded rendition.

10. *Keep all sections of the choir busy during rehearsal, insofar as possible.* During most of the rehearsal the choir is working as a unit. Instructions which apply to *all* singers are given and forthwith put into effect by all. It is easy to command the attention of all because each one is directly involved and challenged.

Something quite different occurs when, for instance, the tenor line for a brace or so is unusually difficult. The director must stop and concentrate on the tenors. The other singers, freed for a moment from immediate duty, either sit idly or more frequently engage in more or less audible conversation. This can become quite distracting and can waste many valuable hours in the course of a year's work.

I suggest that the director, after commenting on the occasional necessity for drilling an individual section, request all other singers at such times (1) to maintain silence for a minute or so, so that the instructions can easily be heard by the singers involved, or (2) to hum or sing lightly their own voice parts while the one difficult part is being played or sung, or (3) to sing, an octave lower or higher if needed, the difficult section—all basses, sopranos and tenors, for example, helping the altos with a difficult spot. This scheme fits into Dr. Henry Coleman's admonition:

> To secure really good ensemble, that is to say the fitting together of all the parts into one whole, it is essential that every singer should know *every other part as well as his own.* Only in this way can the whole structure be fitted together perfectly.
>
> The really efficient choir singer is able to keep an eye *on all the other parts,* and sees his own part continually in *relation* to the rest.[9]

These asides to help a particular voice part should be kept brief. If more extensive aid is indicated, have sectional rehearsals for all four voice parts during part of the rehearsal. Or if singers in only one voice part need help, ask them to come early and give them the extra assistance.

11. *Visual aids quicken the learning process.* Successful choir directors are good teachers and know that the learning procedure is speeded by the use of eye as well as ear. Charts prepared beforehand or blackboard diagrams can underline some choral principle. For instance, if a choir scoops up to a pitch, these two figures will

[9] *The Amateur Choir Trainer* (New York: Oxford University Press, 1932), p. 138-39.

sharpen the problem and its solution. When singing this interval leap:

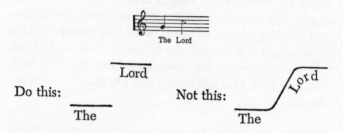

When you read books on choral technique underline salient statements. Copy one of these each week on the blackboard and leave it during rehearsal. Here are some I like:

"The average singer gets too much pace on whenever the notes show tails."—Sir Hugh Roberton, *Mixed Voice Choirs.*

"Time every consonant ⎫ to your team"
Tone every vowel   ⎬   *The Church*
Tune every note   ⎭ *Anthem Book* (Oxford)

"Physicist and musician agree that discord implies motion toward concord."—David Ferguson, *A History of Musical Thought.*

"Strive to unite your voices together so as to make one clear melodious sound."—John Wesley, *Directions for Singing,* 1761.

You can secure an easel and mount a large tablet—two by three feet—on it so that it can be easily read by all singers in the rehearsal room. Consonant and vowel charts and exercises, musical exercises, descriptions of note lengths, maxims, and the like can be written on it at home. It can be preserved and re-used.

12. Use various ingenious methods of teaching music.
A good choir director should be a lifelong student of
teaching methods. Ideas can be gleaned from chapters
on rehearsal methods in standard choral technique
books.[10] Here are a number of suggestions, and there
are dozens more that you can uncover for yourself.

There are numberless ways of introducing anthems:
(1) With little preliminary comment, you can play over
the anthem, having asked the choir to listen to it. (2)
Have the choir read it at sight with accompaniment. (3)
An excellent way is to start with the words, giving a
résumé of their intent. They can be read aloud by the
choir, noting the rough general accents. Then read them
in the rhythm of the score—still without music—then
chant them on a common chord. Next, forget the words
for a moment or so and tackle the notes, using a nonsense
syllable like "la-la" or "ta-ta." Aim at getting the feel of
the music and the shapes of phrases. Now put words and
notes together and you and your singers will be amazed
at the synthesis.[11] (4) Some directors will introduce a
new anthem by playing a recording before tackling the
learning of it.

It is wise, as a rule, to use teaching procedures which
move from the general to the particular. If, for example—
and heaven forbid!—there should be exactly one half
hour in which to prepare a moderately difficult anthem,
the director must avoid becoming involved in a lengthy
maneuver of polishing a certain final consonant. He must
remember that the first requirement is to get the choir

[10] See Bibliography for listing of books.
[11] This method is described in more detail in the Music Editors'
Preface of *The Church Anthem Book* (New York: Oxford University Press).

through the anthem without foundering. The next goal is that a majority, if not all, of the pitches and time values must be correct; then some general dynamic contours and expressive qualities can be added, et cetera. He should learn to put first things first.

An underlying aim in teaching methods is the development of self-confidence in each singer. This is produced by repeated successful experiences. Joy and abandon in singing come with assurance based on solid achievement. This acquisition may be hastened by clever use of unaccompanied singing. At first, several choral responses or "Amens," already well learned, could be sung without accompaniment—or perhaps with just the bass melody lightly thickened by the accompaniment. Next, try a familiar hymn in four parts, accompanying the choir on every other phrase. Finally, try an unaccompanied anthem in three stages, first with accompaniment, next with a very light accompaniment, and finally, with the choir on their own. Do not be concerned with or mention a slight falling in pitch. Later, when assurance is stronger, you can try to re-inforce a sense of key-tone memory.

In teaching a certain section of melody which lies very high in pitch it is helpful at first to drop it an octave into a more comfortable range for the singers. Then, when the accurate pitches and time values have been established, the snatch of melody can be returned to the original range and anchored.

You will want to show your choir different styles of singing. Basic in the vocabulary is the smooth legato flow. Then there are the light, crisp, or completely staccato items. Intense outpourings in crescendi should be mastered. These varied styles can be caught more easily by hearing a recording by a top choral group like Robert Shaw's or Roger Wagner's.

An organist-director can add variety and efficiency to rehearsal by engaging a competent pianist—upon occasion or permanently—to take over at the keyboard while the conductor gives undivided attention to the singers. (Of course, you will let the pianist know just what music is to be used, especially if his sight reading is not superlative.) The conductor can thus walk around, listening, singing with, and encouraging the choir. If the anthem has an independent accompaniment—its music completely different from the voice parts—it is very wise to have the accompanist play over the voice parts when the music is first tackled. When these are mastered the independent lines of the accompaniment can be added quietly. In outlining a melody for director and singers, the accompanist can sometimes make the pitches clearer by playing them in octaves. An experienced accompanist can foresee difficult passages in the various voice lines and can thicken these to impress them on the minds of the singers.

There is an expedient if you cannot find an accompanist. Pre-record accompaniment on tape—with a metronome ticking into the mike—and use this as accompaniment.[12]

The director should not hesitate to sing to the choir to illustrate a certain desired tonal effect. He should not be deterred because he does not have an excellent voice, but should be willing to sing because his work requires it. This type of vocal illustration will save much time. To help understand this principle, one can imagine an art instructor with a class of students in front of him. In

[12] Choral directors can secure much help by reading Frederick Franz, *Metronome Techniques,* foreword by Dr. Howard Hanson (New Haven, Conn., 1947).

trying to communicate a certain curve of color he does not say, "The line begins almost imperceptibly on the left of the canvas about an inch from the edge, rises and widens to the top center, then abruptly dips and narrows. The line is an unusual blend of orange and green." No. He simply dips his brush upon his palette and with a single flowing stroke he illustrates to his class the intended curve and color. Just so a director must be ready and able to demonstrate with his voice the precise melodic shape or vowel color required. Most good conductors do this much of the time.

The director constantly teaches sensitivity to blend and balance. His ideal is a vital, rich tone which conveys the words with unerring clarity. In a four-part mixed choir this implies individual sections (S, A, T, and B) in which the separate voices merge in a fine blend. On the one hand, no single voice protrudes; on the other hand, voices do not stay mousily in the background contributing little or nothing. Each voice, well produced, retains its own individuality and is not sacrificed to produce a dull homogeneity of choral tone. To accomplish this blend each chorister must possess some skill in basic tone production and in the formation of pure vowel colors. As the British choirmasters are fond of advising, choir singers should listen to themselves, to their fellows, and to their accompaniment.

Have a small box of pencils near the entrance of the practice room and urge each person to have one all during rehearsal. They are great boons for the inevitable memoranda to be added to anthem scores. No minds are adhesive enough to recall all the director's comments and instructions. Four check marks over a whole note will remind the singer to feel the four pulsations and to hold the note full value. Add breathing marks, slurs to carry over ends of phrases, circles around pitfalls. In more elaborate scores it is sometimes difficult in turning pages to find which staff belongs, say, to the bass section. An arrow penciled in takes the eye to this spot immediately.

When the going gets tough, learn to divide and conquer. Remember that a group of singers, attacking an anthem the first time, is doing a good many things simultaneously—reading words, pitches, time values, volume, and interpretive indications; tuning with neighbors; and trying to keep an eye on you. As suggested above, you can lay aside pitch and words for the time being and concentrate on the rhythmic aspect. With feet tapping or hands clapping—or both—to mark the steady pulse of the time movement, the singers can "ta-ta-ta" the time values of their individual voice parts. When these are fastened in their minds, add the words in rhythm. Then add the pitches. Incidentally, many choir directors teach the basic time-beating patterns (given in Chap. V) to the choir, and the singers are invited to use them, in miniature form, while they are rehearsing. This custom is a boon, especially in singing correct time patterns.[13]

One of the most important skills you can instill in your singers is the ability to maintain a steady constant sense of the pulsation of the music. "Never stop the *march of the song*," Plunkett Green wrote.[14] Many tricks can be used. Sometimes the conductor can count out loud, with the singers clapping their rhythms and the accompanist playing his part. Half the choir can count aloud while the other half sings their notes and claps simultaneously —with accompaniment playing too. In this connection,

[13] Howard Shanet has excellent sight-reading techniques in *Learn to Read Music* (New York: Simon & Schuster, Inc., 1956).
[14] *Interpretation in Song*, p. 37.

you must help them to develop the habit of releasing the final note of a phrase in time to breathe and begin the next phrase right on the beat. This frequently means clipping this final note by a fraction. Some composers write in rests for such breath refueling; others may add apostrophes, but many do neither. Another by-product of keeping this steady beat will be seen in crisp simultaneous enunciation of final consonants. Composers like Vaughan Williams assist this by scoring their phrase endings as in this example from "O how amiable." On the word "God" the choir feels four quarter note pulses and enunciates the D on the fourth beat.

My   King_____ and   my   God._____

Used by permission of Oxford University Press.

Another of Plunkett Green's rules for song interpretation is helpful in teaching anthems. He says, "Sing mentally through your rests." [15] In the majority of anthems singers are not busy from beginning to end. Usually there are brief instrumental preludes, interludes, and postludes. Furthermore, there may be solo sections or divisions of labor so that there are a number of spots when a given singer is silent. It is precisely during these moments that this singer must "sing mentally." He must keep the pulse going and the melody, or melodies, sung or played by others must pass through his mind. Since it is difficult, for example, for the average singer to read at sight and to follow mentally some of the organ introductions, I frequently play the main theme of these bars and have

[15] *Ibid.*, p. 92.

the choir "la-la" the tune in unison and go from this into their first notes. Then I ask them to hum these bars lightly while I play it. Finally they can do it mentally. This insures a clean confident attack and gets us off the ground neatly.

I want to emphasize again the value of going from slow to fast, especially when teaching beginning choristers. The experienced singer can glance at a phrase like:

and in a flash compare it with hundreds of similar or identical patterns stored in his musical memory and then sing it perfectly. His musical vocabulary is rich. The beginner, alas, has no such reservoir. It is as foolish to take him through the music up to speed the first time as it is to take a novice auto driver up on the Skyline Drive in Virginia and tell him to admire the scenery in the lovely Shenandoah Valley below him. Unless he keeps his mind on the road, the foot pedals, the dashboard, and the mechanics of driving, he may be in the valley by the short way!

13. *Give instructions in brief, exact, and vivid statements.* Develop economy of expression. Learn to eliminate the "uhs" which stack up between phrases, clauses, and sentences. Do your thinking while the choir is singing. If necessary, write down some of the usual instructions in brief form. As Francis Bacon said, "Writing maketh an exact man." [16] Urge the choir to refrain from side comments as soon as they finish singing a section. Have instructions for them immediately.

When you are not returning to the beginning of the

[16] From his "Essay on Studies."

anthem, learn to find the most efficient starting point. The top of the page is frequently a clumsy starting point. A few editors mark divisions A, B, or C or will number every five or ten measures. Beginnings of sections are usually easier to get into. When indicating a starting point, always give page number first, then the line, then the measure, and finally the beat. Do this sufficiently slowly so that you indicate the line just as they have found the page. You will save much time by this method. If you say, "Begin at the third measure," the choir would have a right to say, "There are dozens of 'third measures' in the piece. Which one?"

It is so easy to become pedestrian in our interpretive comments—"Get a little louder at the top of the page" or "Slow down." Recently I made a few notes during rehearsal led by a top choral person in the country. Here are some sample comments. To overcome sluggishness, she said in a deep, vital voice, "Let's go, you people. Get with it!" To get the singers' heads out of their music, she simply said good-humoredly, "I'm still here," and, later, "Look away. We're memorizing." When the choir gasped audibly during inhalation she remarked, "I shouldn't hear you breathe." When they managed to improve on a phrase she complimented them with "Much better!" When the choir was singing too casually and thinly, she admonished, "Not loudly but deeply! Get your roots down and anchor. Sing with conviction." To get a firm attack on the first beat of a 4/4 measure, she counted with a deep, vibrant tone, "Two and three and breath - ing sing!" [17]

[17] In this connection, read Dr. Henry Coward's pages on "catch-words" and "motto words," *Choral Technique and Interpretation* (London: Novello and Company, Limited), pp. 273-76. He has excellent suggestions about directors' comments to choirs.

14. *In rehearsal, refrain from singing continuously with the choir. Listen to and watch the singers.* The basis of choral progress is the awareness of tonal errors and the application of corrective measures. Granted that it may be expedient for the director occasionally to sing with a section, as a rule he should listen keenly. If you must sing during an emergency absence of a chorister, be sure you blend with the others. Do not let your anxiety that the anthem "go over" lead you to force your voice. A leading choral conductor once told me that he learned about as much by watching a choir as by listening. You can determine how well a section or a person knows the music by noting facial expressions and lip movements.

15. *Rehearse the choir in the loft or chancel at some time during the practice if rehearsal is held in another room.* I prefer to rehearse my choir in a special practice room. Not only is the sanctuary frequently unheated during a portion of the year, but directors usually find that notes can more readily be taught with the percussive outlining accompaniment of the piano than with the organ. In the choir room they get used to the piano and the acoustics of the smaller room. Because the church acoustics, physical arrangements, and instrument are quite different, it is extremely wise to take the choir into the church for a final check on Sunday's music. In chilly weather, when the church is unheated, I reserve the last ten minutes of weekday rehearsal for church practice. The singers could put on their winter outer garments and not be uncomfortable in a cold church.

16. *End the rehearsal on time with a bracing well-learned number.* Few traits so endear a director to a choir as the ability to terminate rehearsal on time. Sometimes someone is waiting outside to pick up the singers, or they have bus schedules to meet. And singing an

91

anthem thoroughly mastered leaves a good taste in the singers' mouths.

After Rehearsal

17. *Study the accomplishments and problems of each rehearsal.* Many surgeons write copious postoperative notes. In this manner they crystallize their ideas of their accomplishments, outline the problems, and clarify their understanding of this particular malady. In like manner, choral directors who desire to grow in technical skill must review each rehearsal to discover strong and weak points. A tape recording of the entire rehearsal will be as much help to the conductor as a motion picture of a football scrimmage is to the coach. Sometimes it is wise to ask an experienced choir member to make suggestions regarding practice routine. One need not ask the whole choir to sit in judgment upon one's work, nor is it sensible to appear completely uncertain about one's abilities, but there is no harm in seeking and taking intelligent advice from those who are interested in the choir.

18. *It is smart to attend rehearsals led by other successful directors and to watch their tactics.* The printed word simply cannot take the place of a workshop situation. After permission has been granted, visit a rehearsal —choral or orchestral. You will find that eye and ear absorb much about the psychology of working with people, and about gestures, tone quality, and interpretive comments.

Dr. Archibald Davison of Harvard succinctly states the real spirit of a successful rehearsal:

To the conductor, concerts may well be no more than exciting interruptions of the processes by which the powers of his chorus are developed. It is at rehearsals that the real work is done. There the conductor learns the capacities of his singers, develops these capacities by ingenuity and persuasiveness, and establishes one half of a reciprocating relationship out of which may grow the final realization of his musical ideals. There the chorus, not on parade, grows into a corporate artistic individuality, stands on terms of real intimacy with the music, penetrates into its true significance, and learns how to make the composer's message eloquent and moving. Indeed, for the singers, too, as well as for the conductor, I am sure it is the rehearsal and not the concert that most often spells adventure.[18]

[18] *Choral Conducting* (Cambridge, Mass: Harvard University Press, 1940), pp. 43-44. Used by permission.

CHAPTER IX

The Choir's Music

Recently, out of curiosity, I measured the thickness of the pile of anthems which had accumulated on my study shelves. There was a stack five feet high! Thousands of separate anthems! Many of them are transitory, meretricious, but hundreds are superb and, consequently, enduring.

An inquiring choir director becomes almost overwhelmed as he digs farther into the heap of choral riches. He knows that an enormous wealth of music is available —profound theological texts beautifully phrased with music of rare craftsmanship. He finds fascinating newness in music coming from the pens of contemporary American and European composers, and the more he explores the sacred choir music of history the greater becomes his amazement. If, for example, he should make a special study of a master composer like Heinrich Schütz, he perceives the keen authenticity with which this immortal sets forth biblical passages.

You will understand the predicament if you imagine that you are the director of a brand-new art museum. A wealthy benefactor has given you funds to purchase one hundred paintings. By a large stretch of imagination, suppose all the paintings existing in New York City at the moment were gathered into a large warehouse for your perusal and purchase. All of the famous galleries were emptied and their contents placed in this warehouse. Each art class sent all the products of its students.

Myriads of canvases—good, bad, indifferent—were there, unmarked, and you knew it. What basis for judgment would you use? Would your final choice include only the immortals?

Faced with the enormity of choral literature—and assuming limited choir directorship experience—what are some considerations which can guide you?

1. *Pursue excellence.* Judgment of excellence is a personal decision of each director. No two directors would be apt to agree on the superior quality or the demerits of every piece of music. This taste for the superlative develops as the innate integrity, ideals, and artistic experience of each person is deepened and broadened. Percy Scholes stated it this way:

It would appear that the first duty of any church musician is the acquirement of a standard of musical taste—which means the thoughtful acquaintance with a large and varied body of all that music which time, the only infallible critic, has endorsed. It should be emphasized that simplicity and elaboration are not the same thing as bad and good. The decision as to simple or elaborate music in a church is one to be made on purely practical grounds, the decision as to bad or good being, on the other hand, essentially a moral question. Much of the simplest music in use is perfectly strong and good, and much of the most elaborate is extremely weak and poor—the converse being likewise true. The effort to improve the music in any particular church has too often taken the line of adding to its elaboration instead of that of raising its quality.[1]

The text, the music, and the matching of both should come under constant scrutiny. Some watered-down texts,

---

[1] *The Oxford Companion to Music,* p. 166. Used by permission.

for example, seem to be couched in terms so general as to be useful in a conservative evangelical congregation, a Unitarian church, or a Buddhist temple. The publisher could certainly sell more of these copies. Should not the text rather have solid theological content and logical development to challenge the listener to attention? If the words deal with the love of God, we should not dare to use the language of sickly sentimentality. Old favorites need reappraisal. Erik Routley's probing mind questions Stainer's use in Chorus 18 of the *Crucifixion* of the words, "From the throne of His Cross the King of grief cries out to a world of unbelief, Is it nothing to you, all ye that pass by?" Routley asks, "Is that self-pitying misapplication of a text from Lamentations tolerable as an imagined utterance of the Lord who reigns from the Tree?" [2] Contrast this text used by Stainer with the exalted conceptions expressed by Isaac Watts and Charles Wesley in their hymns on the Passion of our Lord.

In the music, the thematic material must be freshly alive, beautiful, vocally appropriate. Organic growth, unity, and balance must be manifest throughout. Each of the voice parts should be significant and should yield harmonies appropriate to the textual and musical meaning at the moment. In place of clichés denoting either dryness of inspiration, haste of writing, or poverty of

[2] *Music, Sacred and Profane*, p. 59. After a recent visit to the United States, Dr. Routley observed (*The British Weekly*, September 13, 1962), ". . . with all this interest in church music . . . there is virtually no consciousness of the words to which music is sung: . . . There is a gap between the love of music and the intelligent appreciation of words. There is a gap between the ability to sing Brahms and Byrd and the question whether these ought to be sung at all."

craftsmanship, there should be freshness and vitality expressive of the Christian Gospel.

When John Calvin stated in his Foreword to the Genevan Psalter that the songs to be used in public worship should have "weight and majesty" he was indicating that both words and music must reflect the glorious nature of Almighty God.

2. *Expand your musical and textual vocabulary.* Insofar as the anthems reflect the faith of your denomination, find the best of *all* ages and styles and use them. Do not ride a hobby of one kind; for example, music issued by one publisher or music by only one composer. If you have steered—consciously or unconsciously—away from contemporary music, get Leland Sateren's *The New Song: A Guide to Modern Music for Use in the Church Choir.*[3] With this aid you can begin exploration of this fascinating area.

Make a project of going through each anthem in a well-balanced collection. A good example is *The Oxford Easy Anthem Book.* It was developed by a committee of the Church of Scotland, with Herrick Bunney, organist at St. Giles Cathedral, Edinburgh, as musical adviser. The fifty anthems come from such diverse composers as Palestrina (*ca.* 1525-94), Dering (*ca.* 1550-1630), J. S. Bach (1685-1750), Arne (1710-78), Mozart (1756-91), and Mendelssohn (1809-47). Naturally contemporary British writers predominate. A study of this anthology —or of *The Church Anthem Book* (Oxford), which contains one hundred anthems—will bring a cross section of first-rate choral literature within your ken.

3. *Select music graded to your skill and that of your choir.* Just as a public school curriculum is graded to fit

[3] Minneapolis: Augsburg Publishing House, 1958.

the intellectual background and attainments of the students, so an astute director will select music adapted to the general competence of his choir. One of his goals is to develop the free singing spirit in each of his choristers. This can occur only if they develop technical confidence based on solid artistic achievement.

Having said this, shouldn't we acknowledge that we frequently select the easy way out? Read what Erik Routley said:

> Getting too much too easily is, in ordinary human relations, dangerous. It leads to superficial thinking and speaking, to the debasement of reason and the relaxation of proper self-discipline; and in the end to sentimentality which is own brother to cruelty. . . . They would rather sing a corny anthem weekly than one which demands a month's practice monthly.[4]

Give the choir anthems which challenge them to grow. It may take more than the usual four to five weeks to master them. You may need to devise new ways of teaching subtle rhythmic problems or melodic intervals. Occasionally you may find that you have assigned an anthem which proves too tough for the nonce. Lay it aside and re-introduce it several months later or next season. It may be quite manageable then. What they do now, let them do well.

This is not to say that simple music is out of place. As Scholes observed above, some of the greatest music is not complex. This simplicity requires artistry and devotion for proper rendition.

Remember that adaptiveness—within the composer's intent—can eliminate some technical problems and permit the use of some anthems which otherwise would be

[4] *The British Weekly* (December 29, 1960).

impossible to sing. For example, if a stanza of an anthem is beyond the present ability of the whole group of singers, a quartet of the best readers might properly be given this section. A division marked "unaccompanied" can be handled when the organist gives a light, almost imperceptible support—without sixteen-foot tone.

4. *Select music appropriate to the church year and also to the specific moment in the particular church service.* Increased observance of the calendar of the Christian year furnishes a means of correlating anthem choice with the principal theme of the service. An abundant choral literature based on this liturgical pattern is available. *The Easy Anthem Book,* described above, has a special index of its anthems arranged according to the church seasons.

Not only is there shape and meaning in the yearly worship of the church but there should be logic and orderly progression in each service. The only justification for any musical expression in a service should be the fact that at that moment it is the perfect expression for the congregational thought and emotion. Never should it be irrelevant and distracting. It should gather and give utterance to each motion of the spirit within the worshipers.

Types of choral music used by church singers range in size from single and manifold settings of "Amens" and brief liturgical items, through anthems and motets, to major choral works of considerable dimension. In *Planning for Church Music* the following suggestions, somewhat expanded, of means of becoming acquainted with a wider literature for choirs are given:

1. Study anthems which are suggested by qualified church musicians. . . . Lists of excellent anthems for adult choirs, graded as to difficulty (easy, more difficult), are found in

Lovelace and Rice, *Music and Worship in the Church,* pp. 133-38. . . . [Nashville: Abingdon Press, 1960.]

2. Some publishing houses provide an anthem examination service by means of which a selected group of a dozen or so anthems is mailed to a customer. After these are studied for several weeks, they may be purchased or returned to the publisher. . . . Two publishing houses which maintain unusually high quality in type of anthems included in these packets are The Methodist Publishing House through its Cokesbury Book Stores, and Concordia Publishing House, St. Louis 18, Missouri.

3. Some church music periodicals issue anthems bound within the covers. Among them are *Music Ministry* of The Methodist Church and the *Journal of Church Music* of the Lutheran Church. . . .

4. Occasionally directors pay informal visits to fellow church musicians and look over new music with them. . . .

5. Chapters of the American Guild of Organists occasionally devote a monthly meeting to anthem reading. . . .

6. Publishers of church choral music are glad to put an active director on their mailing lists to receive lists of anthems and frequently they send review copies of the octavo anthems or reduced scores of this music.

7. If a local music store has an enterprising choral manager, it is possible to browse through his files and decide on usable titles.[5]

Because of limited space, I have listed only twenty anthems which could be mastered by many amateur choirs.

[5] Sydnor, *op. cit.,* pp. 76-78.

J. S. Bach (Arr. Harris)	King of Glory, King of Peace (A beautiful extended chorale. Will demand work.)	Oxford
Bechler	O the blessedness is great (From the Moravian Music Series. Three stanzas with identical music. Gracious and simple.)	H. W. Gray MCM #12
Davis	As it fell upon a night (Both text and tune are in the Episcopal *Hymnal 1940*. An adroit arrangement according to needs of each of the six stanzas.)	Galaxy Music Corp. #1819
Davison	Thy wisdom, Lord, all thought transcendeth (A simple, effective setting of the Russian folk melody found in many hymnals under tune name "St. Petersburg."	E. C. Schirmer #1703

101

Friedell	Jesus so lowly	H. W. Gray #2018
	(The late organist of St. Bartholomew's in New York has sensitively and economically set this fine text. Beautiful vocal writing.)	
Holst (Arr.)	Christmas Song (Unison)	G. Schirmer #8119
	(A stunning Nativity anthem with outstanding chime effect accompaniment.)	
————	Let all mortal flesh keep silence	Galaxy #5
	(A widely-used, not-too-difficult arrangement of this ancient text [fifth century] and French folk melody.)	
Joubert	Torches	Novello MT 1316
	(A fascinating brief contemporary canticle of Christmas joy.)	
Lovelace	I sing the almighty power of God	Canyon Press
	(A very easy, good wedding of Isaac	

Watts' words with an English folk tune, "Forest Green.")

_____ What shall I render to Canyon Press the Lord
(Dr. Lovelace combines effectively a lesser known Charles Wesley text with an early American folk melody.)

Parry-Coleman Jesus, Lover of my Oxford E 45 soul
(One of the best of the Oxford Easy Anthem Series. Music is the Welsh hymn melody "Aberystwyth.")

Shaw, G. Worship (Unison) Novello #1
(A stirring festival setting of Whittier's brotherhood hymn "O brother man, fold to thy heart thy brother." Also available in four part version.)

Shaw, M. Go forth with God Oxford C. W.
(Unison with Desc.) #191
(A challenging two-part anthem on the

103

theme of personal and corporate dedication.)

Sowerby	Cradle Hymn	H. W. Gray
	(An exquisite, quiet Christmas anthem on Watts' "Hush, my dear, lie still and slumber.")	#2492
————	The snow lay on the ground	H. W. Gray
	(A gay, rollicking folk melody, skillfully set by the dean of American church composers.)	#2240
Terry	Richard De Castre's Prayer to Jesus	Curwen #8624 MZE
	(A lovely modal setting of this ancient prayer.)	
Thatcher	Come, ye faithful	Oxford EA #11
	(Another good Oxford University Press easy anthem with Easter text.)	
Thiman	King of Glory, King of Peace	Novello MT #1049
	(One of this popular English composer's best.)	

Tomblings	Firmly, I believe and truly	Ascherberg, Hopwood & Crew, Ltd.
	(A skillful anthem on Cardinal Newman's trinitarian text.)	
Willan	Here are we in Bethlehem	Oxford W #9
	(An earlier modal anthem by the famous Canadian composer.)	

CHAPTER X

The Choir at Worship
with the Congregation

We repeat that the purpose of the choir's existence
and all its preliminary work is to join with the rest of
the congregation in offering worship to Almighty God
and, in so doing, to lead the congregation in worship
in hymns, anthems, and sung portions of the liturgy.

Physical Arrangements

The choir's participation and leadership will be much
more effective if attention is paid to provision of certain
physical arrangements. Obviously these matters can be
better attended to when planning a new edifice, but much
improvement can be achieved by alterations of existing
facilities.

I have written in greater detail about these matters
elsewhere.[1] There such aspects as the large importance of
acoustics, the planning and purchase of a pipe organ,
and the location of the choir and instrument are discussed. We will summarize some essential points.

The choir and organ and console should always be

---

[1] *Planning for Church Music*, Ch. III, "Music in Corporate
Worship." See also Leo Beranek's important treatment in *Music,
Acoustics and Architecture* (New York: John Wiley & Sons, Inc.,
1962).

located in a compact arrangement close to one another according to these few general principles:

1. The tone of both choir and organ should move in a direct line of sight to each worshiper. The sound will have more authentic quality and ampler volume when it does not have to be reflected at an angle from the walls in order to reach the ears of the people.

2. The choir members should be seated so that all singers can easily hear one another and the accompanying instrument. Especially important are the reflective qualities of the walls, ceiling, and floor of the choir loft or chancel. Carpets, cushions, absorbent ceiling squares, all soak up the tone and prevent its projection. Hard reflective surfaces enable the choir to produce purer, more unforced tones because they are inwardly assured that these tones will be faithfully conveyed to the listeners. Thus, strident overblowing is less likely to occur. I cannot overemphasize this point.

3. Each choir member should clearly see the director and organist, whether this be one or two persons. A church may presently have two persons as organist and director; obviously the organist and singers must be able to watch the director. Next year, however, the church may hire one person as organist-director, in which case each singer must be able to see the director when he is seated at the organ console.

4. If a front location is used for the choir, the gestures of the director or organist should be screened from the congregation so that the necessary conducting motions are visible to choristers only. If the congregation must see the director, he should reduce the size of his gestures so that they are as unobtrusive as possible.

5. If possible the choir space should be so arranged that expanded choral forces could be accommodated. In

many churches a number of choirs are combined upon occasion, and it greatly improves their performances if they can be seated effectively in the choir loft or chancel.

6. Many choir directors prefer that movable posture-supporting chairs be used in rear balcony locations so that a more flexible seating plan is possible. This is especially helpful when additional instruments and/or choirs are used in a service. Pews are customary in a chancel.

7. Racks to hold sheet anthems, anthem books, and hymnals are standard equipment.

8. Adequate lighting should be provided for clear legibility of music text.

It goes without saying that the choir space should be kept in order. Either the sexton or some choir personnel should have this responsibility. There is a definite correlation between the neatness of the physical surroundings of a choir and the precision and orderliness of the singing. A messy, disheveled environment tends to breed carelessness in music making.

Pre-Service Rehearsal

Just as a baseball pitcher must warm up in the bull pen or as orchestral players create quite a din as they loosen up before concert, so a choir should have a few minutes to check over the anthem and to receive any last-minute instructions. The music can lose some of its keen edge between Thursday night and Sunday morning. This can be restored by the pre-service practice.

First of all, recognize that if choristers are well instructed in the mechanics of each service, they will be better able to worship with quiet minds. If, for example, during the service they must whisper to each other to discover which choral music is coming next it distracts singers and congregation alike.

Entering and Leaving the Sanctuary

Several ways of entering and leaving choir spaces are in use. Probably the more frequently used manner is to have the choir walk slowly and quietly into the choir stalls during the prelude and, when all have reached their places, sit together. Some choirmasters have their choirs come in a few minutes before the prelude is completed, in order that they and the congregation may prepare for worship together. The more usual method, no doubt, is to have the choir and clergy enter at the same time. At the end of the service, at the conclusion of the benediction, the choir then turns in orderly manner and leaves the choir space by the nearest exit.

We do not have the space to go into the liturgical meaning of processions.[1] If authorities in a congregation choose to have choir and clergy process, there are a few practical suggestions which can be given. If the choir is instructed to march and sing in time to the music, the playing of the hymn must be strictly regular. The interval between stanzas must be so ordered that the choir begins the next without getting out of step. The singers should take shorter steps than usual, putting feet more or less in front of each other in order not to sway, and they should walk in a dignified nonmilitary manner. A more ancient and probably more widely used method is simply to walk in a dignified manner. I have tried both methods and prefer the second. A main reason is that it is simpler and removes anxiety or overconcern from the

[1] Horace Spence in *Praises with Understanding* (Croydon, Surrey, England: The Royal School of Church Music, 1959), discusses this subject briefly in Ch. VIII. Read also Kettring *Steps Toward a Singing Church* (Philadelphia: The Westminster Press, 1948), pp. 265-71.

singers so that they can concentrate on the main business
—praising God.

Regardless of which of these two methods of processing
is used, the singers should be instructed not to begin
singing until they have passed through the doors into
the church proper, otherwise there is danger of the
vestibule or narthex singers getting out of time with the
main body of singers in the nave. Some churches provide
a rank of pipes in the narthex playable from the console.
Others use a small loudspeaker to indicate pitch and pace
of organ playing. A good many directors instruct their
lead singers to begin walking into the nave about half
way through the "play over." Thus when time to sing
arrives, there are enough experienced singers with the
congregation to insure a good start. As the singers walk
down the aisle double file, they should stand tall, hold
their hymnals up, keep their heads directly behind the
singer in front of them, and walk in a straight line. An
arm's length distance between two successive couples
is usually suggested. If the front section of the choir is
slowed up for some reason, the following couples should
not crowd together, but should shorten their steps so
as to maintain the proper distance between the pairs of
singers.

Choir Procedures and Manners

If the choir is located in front of the congregation, it
is especially important that the members recognize that
they are constantly in full gaze of the congregation. This
being so, singers have a particular responsibility to see
that every action is designed to add to the corporate
worship rather than to distract. Fidgeting, adjusting the

hair, staring out at the congregation—these and other poor choral manners should be avoided. Reverent attention to and participation in each act of worship will go far toward insuring a positive influence on the congregation. Expressive countenances in singing and attention to the words of the minister are two specific instances.

When the choir moves, the actions should be dignified and unified. The members should rise together, turn together, start and stop walking together. Horace Spence, in *Praises with Understanding* wrote, "Finally, there is one golden rule of conduct during any and every service, which is well worth remembering, for it is essential ingredient of reverence and dignity. When walking, turning, rising, sitting, kneeling, bowing, or performing any liturgical action—never hurry—never hurry—never hurry." [2]

Instrumental Accompaniment of the Choir

Regardless of whether organ or piano is used for choral accompaniment,[3] a crucial concern should be balance between the voices and instrument. This problem varies enormously because of the different acoustical and architectural arrangements in various sanctuaries. In the case of a pipe organ the ideal arrangement is to have the pipe-case directly behind and slightly above the singers. The director in front of the singers can easily hear and adjust the balance of the two musical forces. This optimum situation is obviously best achieved in a balcony location.

[2] *Op. cit.*, p. 15.

[3] Although piano and organ are the usual accompanimental instruments in church, increasing use is made of a wide variety of other instruments. For aid in their use, read Helen R. Trobian, *The Instrumental Ensemble in the Church* (Nashville: Abingdon Press, 1963).

The problem of balance becomes very complicated, however, when, for instance, the choir is in a chancel location and the organ chambers have their tonal openings directed toward the congregation and not into the chancel. Here the choir cannot easily hear the supporting tone, and the congregation gets too much of it.

If the playing and directing are done by different people the director can form some judgment of the proper balance, not only from his post directly in front of the singers, but also by checking at various places in the sanctuary. If, however, one person is organist-choirmaster the problem is different. If he can secure the assistance of another organist at some rehearsal he can set up certain combinations of anthem accompaniments and check the overall balance from vantage points in the nave of the church. Or the organist-director could use snugly fitting earphones attached to a microphone located half way down the center aisle and in choir rehearsal check the balance directly.

There are many technical aspects to organ accompaniment of choir music which are beyond the scope of this book. Organ accompaniment of choirs is an integral part of private organ instruction. There are books which contain help in developing this skill. There is a section on Keyboard Accompaniment in the Preface to *The Church Anthem Book*. Samuel Walter has a chapter on "Accompanying Vocal Solos and Anthems" in *Basic Principles of Service Playing*.[4] Numerous organ instruction manuals give aid in registration procedures. We will mention two basic considerations, however. First, many anthems have been written for unaccompanied singing. A keyboard

---

[4] *The Church Anthem Book* (New York: Oxford University Press); Walter (Nashville: Abingdon Press, 1963).

score is printed simply to assist the accompanist in rehearsal. If the director feels that some accompaniment of this anthem is needed in performance, then a very light, reticent combination—perhaps without any sixteen-foot tone in the pedal—is used. The choristers feel sustained but the general effect from the standpoint of the listeners is mainly choral tone. Sometimes only one or two choral lines—the bass part, for example—need to be played. On the other hand, there are many beautiful anthems with independent accompaniments. Most of the anthems of Eric Thiman and the choruses from the German *Requiem* of Johannes Brahms are two instances of this type of anthem. The instrumental accompaniment introduces musical material different from the vocal lines and of equal musical worth. In these cases due care should be taken in the matter of registration and volume to see that the listeners get the full import, not only of the voices, but also of the instruments. As examples of excellent balance between instruments and voices, listen to Bach's *Mass in B Minor* recorded by either Robert Shaw or Herbert Von Karajan.

A second consideration is the fact that in the course of the singing of an anthem there is a constant adjustment of volume. Quiet passages should not be covered up by the instrument. When the soloist moves into a lower range there must usually be an adjustment of the instrument volume. Next, select the registration of organ stops on your instrument which gives the clearest ensemble. Avoid fat, muddy tones which cover choral tone.

The Choir and Hymn Singing

Congregational singing is strongly influenced by the singing of the choir.[5] The spirit, the melody, the tempo, are communicated to the congregation by the choir. John Wesley told his followers in 1761, "Attend close to the leading voices and move therewith as exactly as you can." A good general rule is to have all choristers sing only the melody of the first and last stanzas of each familiar hymn and, if the hymn is unknown, sing all stanzas in unison. Rather than have just the sopranos— perhaps only six—outline the unfamiliar melody for a congregation of perhaps four or five hundred people, it is much better to have the reinforcement of all the tenors, basses, and altos on the tune. Many recently edited hymnals have all hymn tunes cast in a key which is comfortable to average voices. The Episcopal *Hymnal 1940* aims at a D to D range.

Choir Responses

Many worship services include musical liturgical expressions such as introits, prayer responses and amens, sung benedictions, and versicles with the Decalogue. Usually these musical items do not have instrumental introduction. Therefore, the giving of the pitch and the prompt confident entry should be rehearsed until the expression is spontaneous. The choir, in repeated practice, should hear exactly the combination of organ stops which will be used to give the quiet pitch and should learn the expected interval of time before the choral attack. Usually a chord, then a moment of silence during

[5] For further information, read Ch. 10, "The Choirs and Hymn Singing," J. R. Sydnor, *The Hymn and Congregational Singing* (Richmond, Va.: John Knox Press, 1960).

which the breath is taken, then the attack, is the routine. The choir should be instructed to listen to the prayer or the preceding section of the service along with the other members of the congregation with their music open in their laps or on the music racks in front of them. Then when the chord is sounded they lift their heads, inhale while watching the director for the attack signal, and sing.

Many denominational hymnals have a section devoted to these brief choral items. For a good independent source of such material see Donald Kettring's *Choral Responses.*[6]

Special Choral Services

In addition to the regular Sunday services of divine worship, most choirs participate in occasional musical services. At these times the choirs can sing music of larger dimension than usual. For assistance in planning these services and for suggested music possibilities see Charles H. Heaton, *A Guidebook to Worship Services of Sacred Music.* Read also Ch. 15, "Choral Services and Multiple-Choir Festivals," in Kettring's *Steps Toward a Singing Church.*[7]

[6] Philadelphia: The Westminster Press, 1962.
[7] Heaton (St. Louis: Bethany Press, 1962); Kettring, *op. cit.*

115

BIBLIOGRAPHY

Adult Choir Training

(Although the following texts are placed in convenient cate-
gories, many of them cover broad areas and may be consulted
for general choral information.)

General Approach

Cleall, Charles. *The Selection and Training of Mixed Choirs
in Churches.* London: Independent Press, Ltd., 1960.

Coleman, H. *The Amateur Choir Trainer.* London: Oxford
University Press, 1932.

Coward, H. *Choral Technique and Interpretation.* London:
Novello & Company, Ltd., 1913.

Davison, Archibald T. *Choral Conducting.* Cambridge, Mass.:
Harvard University Press, 1940.

Grace, H. *Choral Training and Conducting.* London: Novello
& Company, Ltd., n.d.

Heaton, Charles H. *How to Build a Church Choir.* St. Louis:
The Bethany Press, 1958.

Roberton, H. *Mixed Voice Choirs.* London: Paterson's Publications, Ltd., n.d.

Scott, Charles Kennedy. *Madrigal Singing.* London: Oxford
University Press, 1931. Although directed to interpretation of madrigals, this volume is undoubtedly one of the
best books on interpretation of general choral music.

Acoustics and Music

Beranek, Leo L. *Music, Acoustics and Architecture.* New
York: John Wiley & Sons, Inc., 1962.

Analysis of Major Choral Works

Coward, H. *Choral Technique and Interpretation.* London:
Novello & Company, Ltd., 1913. Handel's *Messiah* and
Mendelssohn's *Elijah.*

117

The Musical Pilgrim Series. Edited by Arthur Somervell. London: Oxford University Press. This excellent series of brief books include such titles as: Terry, *Bach: The Passions;* Armstrong, *Mendelssohn's "Elijah";* and Bairstow, *Handel's Oratorio "The Messiah."*

Tovey, Donald F. *Essays in Musical Analysis (Vocal Music).* London: Oxford University Press, 1937.

Young, P. M. *The Choral Tradition.* London: Hutchison & Company, 1962. The best single recent volume on analysis of choral music of major dimensions, it includes such works as Bloch's *Sacred Service,* Stravinsky's *Symphony of Psalms,* and Martin's *Golgotha.*

Anthem Repertoire

Lovelace, Austin C., and Rice, William C. *Music and Worship in the Church.* Nashville: Abingdon Press, 1960. See Chapter VIII, "The Choir's Music."

Service Music and Anthems for the Nonprofesssional Choir. An official publication of the Joint Commission on Church Music of the Protestant Episcopal Church in the United States. Greenwich: The Seabury Press, 1955.

Breathing

Dodds, G., and Lickley, J. D. *The Control of the Breath—an Elementary Manual for Singers and Speakers.* London: Oxford University Press, 1925.

Choir Members' Guide

Halter, Carl. *The Christian Choir Member.* St. Louis: Concordia Publishing House, 1959.

Conducting

Rudolph, M. *The Grammar of Conducting.* New York: G. Schirmer, Inc., 1950.

Boult, Adrian. *A Handbook on the Technique of Conducting.* Oxford: Hall the Printer, Ltd., 1949.

Equipment

Sydnor, James R. *Planning for Church Music.* Nashville: Abingdon Press, 1961.

History of Choral Music

Dorian, Frederick. *The History of Music in Performance. The Art of Musical Interpretation from the Renaissance to Our Day*. New York: W. W. Norton & Company, 1942.

Douglas, W. *Church Music in History and Practice*. Revised and with additional material by Leonard Ellinwood. New York: Charles Scribner's Sons, 1962.

Ellinwood, Leonard. *The History of American Church Music*. New York: Morehouse-Gorham Company, 1953.

Nicholson, S. H. *Quires and Places Where They Sing*. London: Society for Promoting Christian Knowledge, 1943.

Young, P. M. *The Choral Tradition*. London: Hutchison & Company, 1962.

Instrumental Accompaniment

Conway, Marmaduke Percy. *Church Organ Accompaniment*. New York: The Macmillan Company, 1952.

Moore, Gerald. *The Unashamed Accompanist*. New York: The Macmillan Company, 1944. Although written for piano accompaniment of songs, it has many general principles and applications for choral accompaniment.

Trobian, Helen R. *The Instrumental Ensemble in the Church*. Nashville: Abingdon Press, 1963.

Walter, Samuel. *Basic Principles of Service Playing*. Nashville: Abingdon Press, 1963.

Hymnal Use by Choirs

Patrick, Millar. *The Story of the Church's Song*. Revised for American use by James R. Sydnor. Richmond: John Knox Press, 1962.

Sydnor, James R. *The Hymn and Congregational Singing*. Richmond: John Knox Press, 1960.

Notation Reading

Coleman, H. *Five Minutes Weekly—A Sight-Singing Course*. London: Oxford University Press, 1960.

Shanet, Howard. *Learn to Read Music*. New York: Simon & Schuster, Inc., 1956.

Wilson, Harry R. *Sing a Song at Sight*. Minneapolis: Schmitt, Hall & McCreary Company, 1954.

119

Organization and Management

Kettring, Donald. *Steps Toward a Singing Church*. Philadelphia: The Westminster Press, 1948.

Whittlesey, Federal Lee. *A Comprehensive Program of Church Music*. Philadelphia: The Westminster Press, 1957.

Special Music Services

Dickinson, H. A., and C., and Wolfe, P. A. *The Choir Loft and the Pulpit*. New York: H. W. Gray Company, 1943.

Heaton, C. H. *A Guidebook to Worship Services of Sacred Music*. St. Louis: The Bethany Press, 1962.

Use of the Singing Voice

American Academy of Teachers of Singing. For list of publications write Harold C. Luckstone, Secretary, 57 Winter Street, Forest Hills 75, N.Y.

Cleall, Charles. *Voice Production in Choral Technique*. London: Novello & Company, Ltd., 1955.

Greene, H. P. *Interpretation in Song*. New York: The Macmillan Company, 1912.

National Association of Teachers of Singing. For list of publications write Hadley R. Crawford, Secretary, Simpson College, Indianola, Iowa.

Rice, William C. *Basic Principles of Singing*. Nashville: Abingdon Press, 1961.

Scott, Charles Kennedy. *The Fundamentals of Singing*. London: Cassell & Company, Ltd., 1954.

Choral Diction

Marshall, M. *The Singer's Manual of English Diction*. New York: G. Schirmer, Inc., 1953.

General Church Music Books with
Chapters on Choir Training

Davies, W., and Grace, H. *Music and Worship*. New York: H. W. Gray Company, 1925. Chapter V, "The Team Spirit."

Halter, Carl. *The Practice of Sacred Music*. St. Louis: Concordia Publishing House, 1955. Chapters 11 and 12.

Lovelace, Austin C., and Rice, William C. *Music and Wor-*

ship in the Church. Nashville: Abingdon Press, 1960. Chapter VI, "The Adult Choir."

Manual of Church Praise According to the Use of the Church of Scotland. Edinburgh: The Church of Scotland Committee on Publications, 1932. Chapter VIII, "The Choir and Choir Training," by T. C. L. Pritchard.

Routley, Eric. *Music, Sacred and Profane.* London: Independent Press, Ltd., 1960. See especially Section II, "Texts for Church Musicians: Twelve articles from *The Choir.*"

Sydnor, James R. *The Hymn and Congregational Singing.* Richmond: John Knox Press, 1960. Chapter 10, "The Choirs and Hymn Singing."

Children's Choir Training

Ingram, Madeline D. *Organizing and Directing Children's Choirs.* Nashville: Abingdon Press, 1959.

Ingram, Madeline D., and Rice, William C. *Vocal Technique for Children and Youth.* Nashville: Abingdon Press, 1962.

Jacobs, R. K., compiler, *The Children's Choir.* Rock Island, Ill.: Augustana Book Concern, 1958.

—————————. *The Successful Children's Choir.* Chicago: H. T. FitzSimons, 1948.

General Music Reference Books

Grove's Dictionary of Music and Musicians. Edited by Eric Blom. 5th ed., 9 vols. New York: The Macmillan Company, 1954.

Scholes, Percy A. *The Oxford Companion to Music.* New York: Oxford University Press, 1938, 1943.

Periodicals

American Guild of Organists Quarterly, 630 Fifth Avenue, New York 20, N. Y.

Choristers' Guild Letters. (For directors of children's choirs.) Choristers' Guild, Box 211, Santa Barbara, California.

Diapason, The, Suite 817, Fisher Building, 343 South Dearborn Street, Chicago 4, Ill.

Hymn, The. The Hymn Society of America, 475 Riverside Drive, New York 27, N. Y.

Journal of Church Music. (Lutheran.) 2900 Queen Lane, Philadelphia 29, Pa.

Music Ministry. (Methodist.) The Graded Press, 201 Eighth Avenue, South, Nashville 3, Tennessee.

Musical Quarterly. Journal of the American Musicological Society, New York: G. Schirmer, Inc.

Professional Organizations

American Choral Foundation, Inc., 101 West 31 Street, New York 1, N.Y.

American Guild of Organists, 630 Fifth Avenue, New York 20, N. Y.

American Musicological Society, Library of Congress, Washington 25, D. C.

Hymn Society of America, 475 Riverside Drive, New York 27, N. Y.

Music Educators National Conference, 1201 Sixteenth Street, N. W., Washington 6, D. C.

Music Teachers National Association, S. Turner Jones, Executive Secretary, 32 Browning Street, Baldwin, N. Y.

National Association of Teachers of Singing, Registrar, 33 Newberry Street, Boston, Mass.

INDEX